KU-175-708

San Francisco

DIRECTIONS

WRITTEN AND RESEARCHED BY

Mark Ellwood

ROUGH
GUIDES

NEW YORK • LONDON • DELHI
www.roughguides.com

Contents

Introduction to

San Francisco

One of America's most beautiful cities, San Francisco sits on a fog-capped, hilly peninsula bounded by the shimmering waters of San Francisco Bay to the east and the crashing waves of the Pacific Ocean to the west. Whether you're drawn in by the natural setting, or the free-spirited, non-conformist ways for which the city is also famous, you'll find plenty to keep you occupied once there.

▲ City view from Dolores Park

When to visit

San Francisco's climate is among the most stable in the world, with a daytime temperature that rarely ventures more than 5°F either side of 60°F (15°C) but can drop much lower at night. Summer does offer some sunny days of course, but it also sees heavy fog roll in through the Golden Gate to smother the city. Winters bring most of the city's rainfall, sometimes in quite torrential storms. The nicest times to visit are late May and June, when the hills are greenest and covered with wildflowers, or October and November, when you can be fairly sure of good weather and reduced crowds at the major attractions.

The steep streets are lined with picturesque rows of Victorian houses, and the neighborhoods running alongside dotted with sophisticated restaurants, and chic clubs occupying converted warehouses. What's more, there's an almost small town feel to it all – provided you don't mind the hills, nearly every major sight is just a walk or short bike ride away, and if you do, a great old cable car system provides an equally fun way of getting around.

Named for St Francis of Assisi, the city was transformed almost overnight in the 1840s from a sleepy fishing village to a Gold Rush boomtown. The hilly terrain didn't daunt the prospectors who threw up a city here, and the cataclysmic earthquakes and fires (most notably in 1906 and 1989) only seemed to make people more determined to stay.

Those hills have since helped define the city, both by wealth – in general, the higher up you are, the better the views and the bigger

▼ "Painted Ladies," Alamo Square

▲ A view through the Golden Gate Bridge

the rents – and geography, serving to divide up the dense cluster of districts in the northeast corner. Much of the best streetlife is experienced either around here or in iconic, energetic neighborhoods like the Mission, the Castro, and the Haight, smack in the center of the peninsula. Things open up considerably as you move north and west, to expansive parklands and beaches, and lesser-known residential areas in which you can easily stumble across some of the best ethnic food in the city.

The rest of the Bay Area is quite varied and offers a good complement to cultured city life. Cross the Golden Gate Bridge north to the rocky Marin Headlands and undisturbed Muir Woods for a fine natural escape; further on, the wineries of Napa and Sonoma valleys offer more indulgent pleasures. East of the city, Berkeley is dominated by its university, which has given rise to a thriving bookstore and café scene, and sits just north of the gritty port city of Oakland.

San Francisco
AT A GLANCE

▲ Russian Hill

THE "HILLS"

What San Francisco is probably best known for – Nob, Telegraph and Russian hills form a tight, picturesque nucleus in the city's northeast corner. Come here for views, quiet leafy streets and a brisk bout of exercise hiking up the steep sides.

NORTH BEACH

Next door to teeming Chinatown in the city center, this Italian-American enclave and old beatnik haunt is still replete with delis, restaurants, and cafés serving excellent espresso as well as a burgeoning hipster contingent of stores and funky bars.

▲ North Beach

FISHERMAN'S WHARF

It may be a bit of an overrun tourist trap, but it does have a few points of irresistible tacky waterfront interest, and it's from here that you can catch the ferry to the prison of Alcatraz.

▼ Fisherman's Wharf

▲ The Mission

THE MISSION

Southwest of downtown, the heart of the city's Latino culture beats here: Mission Street's still heavy on taquerias and knick knack shops, while Valencia Street's now a fusion of Anglo and Latino culture and one of the trendiest strips in town.

THE CASTRO

Just west of the Mission, this neighborhood has long been synonymous with gay activism and pride, as well as the wedding cake-like landmark of the Castro Theatre.

▼ The Castro

CHINATOWN

A tightly packed wedge of markets, shops and restaurants just a stone's throw from downtown's skyscrapers – but a world away, culturally, filled with butchers selling live birds, Canto pop-heavy record stores and dirt cheap dim sum joints.

▲ Chinatown

GOLDEN GATE PARK

The expansive, man-made rectangle of greenery in the western sector is home to a brace of fine museums, including the showstoppingly design-conscious new De Young, and several quiet gardens, each with its own theme.

▲ Golden Gate Park

HAYES VALLEY

A quiet, little-known corner of the city located just east of Haight-Ashbury's tie-dyed emporiums, and a superb place to browse for fashion and funky homewares.

Ideas

The big six

There are a handful of sights that define San Francisco, whether it's highbrow culture, brisk outdoorsiness, or Latin heritage. So however brief your visit may be, these half-dozen landmarks constitute must-see stops for anyone hoping to understand the heart and soul of the city.

▲ Union Square

Downtown's hub may be bordered by alluring retail outlets, but a renovation has transformed it into a stand-alone attraction and a great place to relax with a coffee.

P.67 ▸ UNION SQUARE AND AROUND

▲ SF Museum of Modern Art

This showstopping building by Swiss architect Mario Botta was an instant, crowd-pleasing hit as soon as it opened in 1995.

P.115 ▸ SOMA

▲ Golden Gate Bridge

As much an architectural as an engineering feat, built in 1937, this remains the most beautiful, and arguably the most photographed, bridge in the world.

P.108 ▶ PACIFIC HEIGHTS AND THE NORTHERN WATER-FRONT

▲ Mission Dolores

The oldest building in the city was built by the first Spanish settlers; it's survived more than 200 years in remarkable condition.

P.130 ▶ THE MISSION

▼ Alcatraz

This isolated prison was once home to America's nastiest criminals; today it's a moody and evocative place to linger for an afternoon.

P.101 ▶ FISHERMAN'S WHARF AND ALCATRAZ

▲ Cable cars

No-one should visit the city without taking a ride on these rickety but reliable trams, which vie with the Golden Gate Bridge as the city's most visible symbol.

P.69 ▶ UNION SQUARE AND AROUND

Golden Gate Park

The urban planners who masterminded San Francisco's rapid expansion in the last decades of the nineteenth century were forward-thinking enough to set aside a swathe of land in what was then the city's wild western edge to be a permanent park. That green space still stands today and is filled with a vast range of attractions and distractions.

▲ Japanese Tea Garden

Come sit and sip amid the bonsai trees, statues and pagodas of a turn-of-the-century Japanese garden – in the heart of San Francisco.

P.153 ▶ GOLDEN GATE PARK

▲ Conservatory of Flowers

This recently overhauled, Victorian era hot-house is home to a stunning array of exotic and unusual plants.

P.154 ▸ GOLDEN GATE PARK

▼ AIDS Memorial Grove

A secluded, woodsy memorial garden that was the first of its kind in the country to commemorate victims of AIDS and HIV.

P.155 ▸ GOLDEN GATE PARK

▲ Shakespeare Garden

Use the handy plaque here to count how many plants and flowers the Bard referenced in his works – and then try to find your own favorites.

P.155 ▸ GOLDEN GATE PARK

◀ Strybing Arboretum

Escape the more crowded sections of the park and stroll among the thousands of varieties of plants on display here from all over the world.

P.154 ▸ GOLDEN GATE PARK

Green San Francisco

One of the things that sets San Francisco so far apart from other American cities is its obsession with the outdoors – drive minutes across any bridge on the Bay, and within you're in easy reach of beautiful, strenuous hiking and biking trails. But even within the city itself there are plenty of green spaces perfect for a walk, jog, or a relaxing time in the sun (or fog, as the case may be). Golden Gate Park is the first spot to make for; after that, check out any of the following.

▲ Land's End

Ramblers will enjoy this wilderness park that hugs the cliffs on the city's northwestern tip and overlooks the Pacific Ocean.

P.159 ▸ THE RICHMOND AND THE SUNSET

▼ Washington Square Park

Come here early in the morning to see swathes of elderly local Chinese practicing t'ai chi together.

P.85 ▸ NORTH BEACH

▼ The Presidio

For a break from the bustle of downtown, spend a day ambling round this former military base that's quilted with hiking trails and cycling paths: don't miss the new statue of Yoda outside George Lucas' ILM complex.

P.108 ▶ PACIFIC HEIGHTS AND THE NORTHERN WATER-FRONT

▲ Fort Mason

Schizophrenic, sprawling park and museum complex, with shady nooks by the water and view-blessed open lawns on the top of the hill.

P.101 ▶ PACIFIC HEIGHTS AND THE NORTHERN WATER-FRONT

▲ Dolores Park

The Mission's main green space is perched on the side of a hill and offers rolling views across the city.

P.130 ▶ THE MISSION

▶ Alamo Square

Though the views from the park, perched on a hill, are impressive enough, it's the overlooking row of fastidiously restored Victorian houses that draws shutterbugs.

P.145 ▶ HAIGHT-ASHBURY AND HAYES VALLEY

Chic hotels

Of course, if you want a reliable, if uninspiring, room run by one of the global chains, there are plenty of choices close to downtown. But San Francisco specializes in boutique hotels and quirky guesthouses: if you value a more individualistic experience and local feel, try one of the following, all of which are in or close to the city center. They include two converted schools (one for wayward boys, the other for convent girls), plus a brand new spa-inflected Embarcadero spot and the city's first hotel helmed by artists.

▲ The Mosser

A hotel with three key advantages: a handy location close to Union Square, rock-bottom rates and a funky Modernist-meets-Victoriana vibe.

P.191 ▸ ACCOMMODATION

▼ Queen Anne Hotel

Once a girls' school, and possibly haunted, there's history to spare in this extravagantly decorated hotel in Pacific Heights.

P.191 ▸ ACCOMMODATION

▼ Hotel Vitale

Vaguely spa-themed hotel with comfy beds and terrific Bay views; the chance to spot former Mayor Willie Brown in person every morning when he broadcasts his breakfast show from here is a plus.

P.191 ▸ ACCOMMODATION

▲ Hotel des Arts

Hybrid art gallery-cum-hotel with rooms decaorted by local artists as well as pictures for sale hung all over the lobby's stark white walls.

P.189 ▸ ACCOMMODATION

▶ Archbishop's Mansion

Every room at this luxurious B&B on Alamo Square – actually built in 1904 for the city's new archbishop – is named after an opera and decorated to match.

P.192 ▸ ACCOMMODATION

Gay San Francisco

An estimated one in every five locals is either gay, lesbian, bisexual or transgender, so San Francisco more than earns its unofficial ranking as the most gay-friendly destination in the world. From dance clubs to sex clubs, from sites of protest to sights of progress, there's nowhere better to understand the history of gay liberation – or to get dressed up and strut down the street with pride.

▲ Dolores Beach

On a hot summer weekend, this patch of the Dolores Park is a splendid place to lay out and catch some sun – and a little attention.

P.130 ▸ THE MISSION

▲ Harvey Milk

The first openly gay local politician passed permanently into the history books when, along with mayor George Moscone, he was assassinated in City Hall by a disgruntled ex-colleague.

P.125 ▸ THE TENDERLOIN AND CIVIC CENTER

▲ The Stud

Bar-club that's a legendary, longtime local hangout, best on Tuesday's fabulous drag-inflected freakshow, "Trannyshack".

P.122 ▸ SOMA

▶ The Castro

This neighborhood is to San Francisco what the city is to the rest of the country: the epicenter of gay culture.

P.138 ▸ THE CASTRO

▼ GLBT Historical Society

Tucked away on the third floor of a Soma office building, this archive/exhibition space is the only such spot in town dedicated to gay and lesbian local history.

P.113 ▸ SOMA

Local labels

This may be the city that turned the world blue and khaki one pair of pants at a time (thanks to the Gap and Levi's, which were both founded here), but there's much more to shopping in San Francisco than corporate megastores. We've scoured the streets for the best finds in local labels: pick up a pair of shoes or a pulp paperback at one of these stores, and you can be sure it's a unique souvenir.

TRUE
SAKE

▲ True Sake

A unique, sleek store that sells only Japanese rice wine – more than 100 varieties – and whose owner will happily spend time explaining the subtleties of sake.

P.148 ▸ HAIGHT-ASHBURY AND HAYES VALLEY

▲ Amoeba Records

Vast, warehouse-like music store wedged
into the western end of Haight-Ashbury – the
best place to buy (or sell) music in the city.

**P.146 ▶ HAIGHT-ASHBURY AND
HAYES VALLEY**

▼ Velvet Da Vinci

Gem-like jewelry store-cum-gallery, showcasing a wide range of local designers:
pricey, but a dazzling place to browse.

**P.96 ▶ NOB HILL, RUSSIAN HILL,
AND TELEGRAPH HILL**

▲ Paolo Iantorno

A local shoemaking superstar, Iantorno
designs and produces limited editions of
men's and women's funky footwear for
around $200 per pair.

**P.147 ▶ HAIGHT-ASHBURY AND
HAYES VALLEY**

Museums

The city may not be quite on a par with New York or LA in terms of overall fine arts holdings, but its specialized collections hold their own: bronze maquettes by Rodin, steel ropes running 24 hours a day, and wrought metal money trees, to name a few. Here are five of the best places to pick up a little cultural cachet, including one new hotspot that the whole city's buzzing about.

▲ California Palace of the Legion of Honor

The range and depth of the Rodin holdings here make this, hands down, the most impressive and important museum in town.

▲ Cable Car Museum

Come here to really see how those colorful, rickety cars manage to clamber so nimbly up the city's steep hills.

▶ de Young Museum

A dazzling new addition to the city, the de Young's copper-clad building almost eclipses its own collection.

P.152 ▶ GOLDEN GATE PARK

▲ Asian Art Museum

Crammed with antiquities from every country in Asia, this museum's also notable for the shimmering conversion of an old Beaux Arts building (not to mention its tasty café).

P.126 ▶ THE TENDERLOIN AND CIVIC CENTER

▼ Museum of Modern Art

Highlights of the museum's collection include pieces by the so-called California School (Frida Kahlo and Diego Rivera among others), as well as irreverent oddities from the likes of Jeff Koons.

P.115 ▶ SOMA

Spiritual San Francisco

The first church in town, the Mission Dolores, dates back to 1791, and has remained culturally important ever since – even if it does now share its status as Catholic stronghold with the much more modern St Mary's of the Assumption. In addition to these, a few other places of worship merit a visit on grounds of architectural interest or inviting atmosphere, no matter what your religious beliefs.

▲ Waverley Place temples

It's worth detouring to see the temples hidden here in several old tenements for their combination of old world China and modern Chinatown.

> **P.78** ▸ CHINATOWN AND JACKSON SQUARE

▲ Grace Cathedral

A grand, Neo-Gothic church, gussied up with expensive touches like the reproduction Renaissance panels from Florence, Italy.

> **P.95** ▸ NOB HILL, RUSSIAN HILL AND TELEGRAPH HILL

▲ St Mary's Cathedral

Unfairly derided by many locals for its uncompromising modernist design, this sweeping, curving cathedral's an impressive sight inside and out.

P.105 ▸ PACIFIC HEIGHTS AND THE NORTHERN WATER-FRONT

▼ Mission Dolores

The simplicity of this centuries-old building makes it the most spiritual and welcoming of any church in the city.

P.130 ▸ THE MISSION

▲ Church of St Peter & Paul

Look for the twin turrets that loom over North Beach and mark its spiritual center.

P.86 ▸ NORTH BEACH

Kids' San Francisco

There are few stresses when traveling with kids in San Francisco, other than the tiring hills: most restaurants will welcome young ones and there are reduced rates for almost every attraction or amenity. You can add to all that a handful of sights guaranteed to enchant any child.

▲ Exploratorium

The standout exhibit at this kid-centric science showcase is the sensory-depriving Tactile Dome, a pitch-black romp through touch, taste, smell and sound.

P.107 ▶ PACIFIC HEIGHTS AND THE NORTHERN WATER-FRONT

▼ San Francisco Zoo

Make sure not to miss the zoo's two female Asian elephants, Calle and Tinkerbell, at their daily training sessions at 1.30pm.

P.160 ▶ THE RICHMOND AND THE SUNSET

▲ Ghirardelli Square

Albeit touristy, this is the place where modern chocolate was invented, and it would be a crime not to sample one of the lush, sauce-doused sundaes at the gift shop's café.

P.99 ▸ FISHERMAN'S WHARF AND ALCATRAZ

▼ Golden Gate Park

There's a carousel and a playground here, but this park's equally appealing for its broad green lawns and peaceful calm.

P.152 ▸ GOLDEN GATE PARK

◄ Musée Mécanique

Dozens of arcade games jostle for attention in this buzzing, noisy museum overlooking the water – bring plenty of quarters if you want to enjoy them.

P.100 ▸ FISHERMAN'S WHARF AND ALCATRAZ

San Francisco calendar

As with any major city, celebrations of all sorts happen year round, but things are taken to an extreme here. San Franciscans like dressing up, and they'll jump at any chance to put on a costume – the more outrageous the better. One byproduct of this tendency is that festivals are mostly riotous and all-inclusive affairs; just remember to bring a mask and some makeup if you want to join in.

▲ Halloween

Yet another opportunity for the city's eccentrics to slip into costume, this parade – which usually centers on the Castro – is a marathon of make-up, sequins and scary outfits.

P.202 ▸ ESSENTIALS

▼ Chinese New Year

In late January or early February, both of the city's Chinatowns – downtown and the Richmond – pause for a day to celebrate the arrival of the New Year with a lively parade, street performers and stalls.

P.202 ▸ ESSENTIALS

▲ Gay Pride

Late June each year is the time when San Francisco's LGBT community takes over the streets for a raucous and raunchy parade, though it's the quieter offshoot events in and around the Castro that are often far more fun.

P.202 ▶ ESSENTIALS

▼ Cinco de Mayo

Though only a regional fiesta back in Mexico that commemorates a nineteenth-century victory over the French, this holiday is celebrated by expat Latinos across America – and the Mission is one of the liveliest spots to enjoy it.

P.202 ▶ ESSENTIALS

▲ Cherry Blossom Festival

Japantown's transformed into a riot of pale pink flowers during this springtime festival, which culminates in the selection of a Cherry Blossom Queen.

P.202 ▶ ESSENTIALS

San Francisco specialties

The waves of immigrants who've settled in San Francisco have left their mark on the city – mostly in its menus: in a single day, you can nibble on Cantonese dim sum, recharge with espresso stiff enough for a Roman and gorge yourself on homemade tacos. Even better, you can try the city's homegrown specialties like steam beer, a byproduct of warm days and thirsty early locals, who couldn't afford the ice to brew bitter so fermented their yeast at room temperature and created a brand new beer.

▲ Tacos

You can't leave town without sampling one of these sloppy, cheap, and delicious treats, San Francisco's unofficial snack of choice.

P.134 ▶ THE MISSION

▲ Boudin sourdough bread

For reasons so far unexplained, the yeast that sours this dough can't survive outside the city, so try it while you can.

P.102 ▶ FISHERMAN'S WHARF
AND ALCATRAZ

▲ Espresso in an Italian caffè

Only cowards order cappuccino.

▼ Dim sum

These snack-sized portions are served from trolleys in restaurants across town; ask about any off-menu, insiders' specials.

▲ Steam beer

Don't worry about the watery name – the locally produced brews, known as "steam beers," have the hearty taste of bitter but the lower alcohol content of lager; you can sample it at microbreweries like the *Thirsty Bear*.

Bars

If you want a quiet cocktail accompanied by a soft jazz soundtrack, San Francisco can serve both the music and the martini; if you're more the Red Bull and remix type, there's a couple of brand new bars with both drinks and dancefloors. For everything in between – grungy pubs in the Mission, beatnik hangouts in North Beach – the vast range of drinking spots on offer should more than fill your needs.

▲ The Canvas

Groovy and huge hipster hangout that's a café and gallery by day, and bar and performance venue by night.

P.162 ▶ THE RICHMOND AND THE SUNSET

▼ Madrone Lounge

Club-cum-art lounge with bi monthly art exhibits and a raffish vibe; the vintage juke box is an appealing touch.

P.151 ▶ HAIGHT-ASHBURY AND HAYES VALLEY

▲ Vino Venue

Gimmicky but fun, this is the wine world answer to the automat, with credit card payments and wine dosed by vending machines.

P.120 ▸ SOMA

▼ Li Po's

Raucous, kitschy bar popular with Chinatown locals and used by Wayne Wang as a setting for his movie *Chan is Missing*.

P.83 ▸ CHINATOWN AND JACKSON SQUARE

▲ Harry Denton's Starlight Room

A sophisticated downtown hotel bar, known for its killer martinis and nightly jazzy soundtrack provided by the Starlight Orchestra.

P.75 ▸ UNION SQUARE AND AROUND

▼ Voda

Dressy, label-heavy bar with an impressive list of different vodkas, more than 100 strong.

P.75 ▸ UNION SQUARE AND AROUND

Cultural San Francisco

Of all things – and there are many – that San Franciscans have to brag about, they are most proud of their city's performing arts. With a world-class symphony orchestra and ballet, not to mention a raft of reliably high-quality fringe venues, this is a city that takes the arts very seriously and yet still finds room for more campy, outré entertainment.

▲ Intersection for the Arts

Oldest alternative space in town, with a reliably counter-culture and protest-heavy programming bent.

P.136 ▸ THE MISSION

▲ The Roxie Film Centre

From obscure documentaries about dog shelters to indie festival favorites, the Roxie shows them all thanks to its determinedly anti-mainstream programming.

P.136 ▸ THE MISSION

▼ Beach Blanket Babylon

This sassy satire has been running at Club Fugazi for thirty years but remains as fresh and naughty as ever – and showcases the most astonishing wigs.

P.90 ▸ NORTH BEACH

▲ Yerba Buena Center for the Arts

Downtown venue that's one of the best places in the city to catch avant-garde dance and theatre.

P.121 ▸ SOMA

▲ San Francisco Symphony

The antics of conductor Michael Tilson Thomas may divide critics, but it's undeniable that he's reinvigorated the local orchestra with a program heavy on twentieth-century composers.

P.129 ▸ THE TENDERLOIN AND CIVIC CENTER

Funky food

San Francisco proudly (and somewhat unverifiably) claims to be second only to Paris in the number of restaurants within its city limits; and there's a bewildering selection of cuisines, prices, and atmospheres on offer. To help you navigate, we've singled out five funky favorites that are always a great place to grab a well-priced meal.

▲ Luella

On a leafy Russian Hill strip, this quiet restaurant dishes up delicious, unfussy modern food with a twist – try the coca cola braised short ribs.

P.97 ▸ NOB HILL, RUSSIAN HILL AND TELEGRAPH HILL

▲ Taylor's Automatic Refresher

Post modern riff on a 1950s diner, with mahi mahi fish and chips and mouth-puckeringly thick milkshakes (try the white pistachio)

P.73 ▸ UNION SQUARE AND AROUND

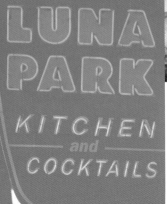

LUNA PARK
KITCHEN
and
COCKTAILS

▲ Nick's Crispy Tacos

Cheap and funky, a taqueria that's as welcoming to local retirees as to sunglass-clad hipsters: don't try to bash the piñata – it's just for show.

P.97 ▸ NOB HILL, RUSSIAN HILL AND TELEGRAPH HILL

▼ Luna Park

A groovy restaurant that attracts a diverse crowd, from young hipsters to older intellectual types, all of whom come for the simple, delicious modern American food.

P.134 ▸ THE MISSION

Cafés

You can still sample some of San Francisco's fabled food even if your budget's more fish and chips than foie gras. Many of the city's cafés can hold their own against more upscale eateries, especially if you want to try exotic or ethnic cuisines in a more relaxed environment where you can feel comfortable lingering. While you slurp that oyster or sip your coffee, you may well be sitting next to one of the city's top chefs, who are partial to the rockbottom prices and sky-high quality of many of the places listed here.

▲ Caffe Trieste

An old school Italian staple in the heart of North Beach, where Francis Ford Coppola is said to have knocked out the first draft of the script for *The Godfather*.

P.87 ▸ NORTH BEACH

▲ Nook

Homey corner café with cheap wines by the glass, tasty sandwiches and plenty of aspiring writers knocking out their screenplays on gleaming laptops.

P.96 ▸ NOB HILL, RUSSIAN HILL AND TELEGRAPH HILL

▼ Swan Oyster Depot

Grab a stool at this cramped but fun seafood café and wolf down the cheap but delicious oysters on offer.

P.97 ▶ THE TENDERLOIN AND CIVIC CENTER

▲ Saigon Sandwiches

A hole-in-the-wall sandwich shop that serves cheap, pork-crammed sandwiches slathered with delicious, sinus-clearing chile sauce.

P.127 ▶ THE TENDERLOIN AND CIVIC CENTER

◀ Café Flore

Cruisey but fun Castro corner café, with an outdoor patio that's ideal for a long, leisurely Sunday afternoon reading the papers and checking out passers-by.

P.141 ▶ THE CASTRO

Late-night San Francisco

If there's one complaint justifiably leveled at San Francisco, it's how early everything closes here; after all, most locals want to be up, out and exercising long before 7am (if they're not already expected in the office by then). For resolute night owls, though, we've picked out the places that are live and kicking well into the early hours – even, in some cases, until those crack-of-dawn joggers start filling the streets.

▲ El Farolito taqueria

The best time to come to this age-old Mission taqueria is late at night, when club kids and late-shift workers sit alongside one another at its refectory tables.

P.133 ▸ THE MISSION

▲ The Globe

Late-night eating doesn't preclude the possibility of fine dining; here you can expect to share drinks or dinner with the dozens of waitstaff from other restaurants who flock here once their shifts end.

P.81 ▸ CHINATOWN AND JACKSON SQUARE

◀ Castro Street

The raucous nightlife here revs up a gear as places elsewhere start closing – and as an added bonus, each bar's no more than a minute's stumble from the next.

P.138 ▶ THE CASTRO

▼ Chinatown night market

Portsmouth Square is a riot of squawking music and crowded stalls when this market's in session, selling everything from clothes to toys and souvenirs.

P.79 ▶ CHINATOWN AND JACKSON SQUARE

▲ Bagdad Café

This diner's definitely a no-frills, no-fuss option but it's one of the few places in town open 24 hours.

P.141 ▶ THE CASTRO

San Francisco for free

Splurged on a five-star meal, and need to save some cash? Want to take home a pricey case of Sonoma chardonnay and have to economize in the meantime? Never fear. There are plenty of ways to see and enjoy the city without once opening your wallet – none of the activities listed here will cost you a penny.

▲ San Francisco MOMA first Tuesday of the month

This is an unmissable local standout – and it's even better to stop by when it's free for everyone.

P.115 ▸ SOMA

▼ Sunday gospel services at Glide Memorial Church

Catch one of the goosebump-inducing gospel services at this charitable church, but make sure to arrive at least two hours in advance for a prime seat.

P.123 ▸ THE TENDERLOIN AND CIVIC CENTER

▶ Baker Beach

Catch some sun on the city's best and cleanest beach, nestled on the peninsula's northwestern rim.

P.159 ▶ THE RICHMOND AND THE SUNSET

◀ Take a City Guides walking tour

Free city tours, run by enthusiastic and chatty amateur historians, on a wide range of topics.

P.200 ▶ ESSENTIALS

▶ Walk across Golden Gate Bridge

It's only when you cross it on foot that you can really enjoy the views of the city as well as understand the sheer, breathtaking scale of the bridge.

P.108 ▶ PACIFIC HEIGHTS AND THE NORTHERN-WATER FRONT

◀ Meditate at the Palace of Fine Arts

It's the stillness and simplicity of the grounds, especially the reflecting pool, which give this doleful holdover from a grand exhibition such power.

P.107 ▶ PACIFIC HEIGHTS AND THE NORTHERN-WATER FRONT

Gourmet San Francisco

It's hard to pinpoint exactly why and how San Francisco's obsession with food began, but many historians point to the Gold Rush. That's when thousands of men swamped the city, took up rooms in boarding houses and demanded a daily meal from the local restaurant. Hordes of eateries appeared in response, and today eating out is still one of the city's number one obsessions.

▲ Jardinière

Chef Traci des Jardins is a local culinary rockstar, and this is her flagship, namesake restaurant: try the six-course tasting menu to see what the fuss is about.

P.128 ▸ THE TENDERLOIN AND CIVIC CENTER

▲ Myth

Beg for a table at this hotspot. Snuggle into a gauzy banquette and thank your grandmother for leaving you an inheritance that will let you pay the bill.

P.82 ▸ CHINATOWN AND JACKSON SQUARE

▲ Molinari's

Old-school deli on the main drag in North Beach, staffed by Italians and decked out with swinging salamis and a smelly, delicious cheese counter.

P.87 ▸ NORTH BEACH

▶ Chez Panisse

Alice Waters, the chef-owner here, is the woman credited with inventing California cuisine, the light, ingredient-driven style of cooking that started in San Francisco and soon spread across the world.

P.170 ▸ BERKELEY

▼ Ferry Building Market-place

Onetime transport hub that's now instead a gourmet nexus, with a farmers market, artisanala produce stores plus first rate cafes and restaurants.

P.73 ▸ UNION SQUARE AND AROUND

▲ Greens

Vegetarian cuisine's big gourmet business in the city, and the poshest place for a plate of portobello mushrooms is Greens, where you can also enjoy the views across the bay to Marin.

P.111 ▸ FISHERMAN'S WHARF AND ALCATRAZ

Sports and the outdoors

Sneakers are the smartest choice of footwear in San Francisco – with so many steep hills to navigate, stilettos are hardly a practical option. But there's another reason everyone should pack a pair of Pumas: the sporting scene. This is an athlete's city, whether you want to catch a game of baseball, skate around a park, or pedal across the Golden Gate bridge; afterwards, you can soothe those aching muscles at a Japanese steam room.

▲ Giants' baseball

The San Francisco Giants' AT&T Park, set right by the water, was built to maximize the home run totals of the great Barry Bonds.

P.117 ▸ SOMA

▼ Rollerblading in Golden Gate Park

Join the hordes of locals who on weekends strap on their blades and slice through the park, from the eastern edge at the Panhandle all the way west to Ocean Beach.

P.152 ▸ GOLDEN GATE PARK

▼ Kabuki Hot Springs

A trendy, converted Japanese bathhouse in the JapanCenter that's a relaxing place to lounge or grab a massage, even for determined spa-phobes.

P.106 ▸ PACIFIC HEIGHTS AND THE NORTHERN-WATER FRONT

▲ Biking around the Presidio

There's no wilder green space in easy reach of downtown, and the vast park here's a struggle to cover on foot; better to rent a bike and cycle its network of looping paths.

P.107 ▸ PACIFIC HEIGHTS AND THE NORTHERN-WATER FRONT

Out of the city

It's easy to take a day-trip out of the city: rent a bike to get across the Golden Gate Bridge, and you'll be in the wilds of the Marin Headlands, or hire a car for a drowsy day around the Wine Country. Berkeley or Oakland are easier options – just 15 minutes' ride by BART– and offer up a nice contrast to each other (and to San Francisco itself): the former quite artsy and freewheeling, the latter a no-nonsense, working-class town.

▲ Bookstores on Telegraph Ave

It's not surprising that a town as student-oriented as Berkeley would have so many bookstores – though it is a pleasant shock that the stock's so wide-ranging and literate.

P.169 ▶ BERKELEY

▲ UC Berkeley campus

The university's surprisingly woodsy and bucolic campus is full of nooks and lawns where anyone's welcome to lounge.

P.167 ▸ BERKELEY

▶ Heinold's First and Last Chance Saloon

A rickety old saloon that's a must-see pilgrimage site for Jack London fans – the writer was a regular.

P.173 ▸ OAKLAND

◀ Oakland Museum

The three-tier exhibition here is a fun and exhaustive look at California's history, ecology and art.

P.174 ▸ OAKLAND

The music scene

Jam bands? A San Francisco invention, thanks to the Grateful Dead. Acid Jazz? The first bands bubbled up in the Bay Area. Post-grunge punk pop? Seattle could only watch Green Day in envy. Little wonder then that the San Francisco music scene today – both live performers and the innovative DJ community – is as vibrant as ever: the venues below are the best places to take its pulse.

▲ Bimbo's 365 Club

Don't be put off by the name – this is one of the most reliable venues for gigs by interesting, big name acts and a few offbeat tribute bands.

P.91 › NORTH BEACH

▲ Mezzanine

Mainstream megaclub downtown with an eclectic playlist and a new stage for occasional live performances.

P.121 ▸ SOMA

◀ Boom Boom Room

Once owned by the late John Lee Hooker, the stage here usually offers fine touring blues and funk performers.

P.112 ▸ PACIFIC HEIGHTS AND THE NORTHERN WATERFRONT

▼ Fillmore Auditorium

Once the hub of San Francisco's counter-culture scene, this large space reopened ten years ago and now hosts regular rock and alt-rock concerts.

P.112 ▸ PACIFIC HEIGHTS AND THE NORTHERN WATERFRONT

▲ Mighty

Onetime warehouse turned art gallery/club; the funk and old school-heavy playlist is a refreshing change.

P.137 ▸ THE MISSION

San Francisco inventions

The pioneering spirit of San Francisco not only fueled the Gold Rush, but made the city home to some major cultural firsts – whether transforming denim from an also-ran fabric from France into a workwear wonder, making going topless a reason for tipping or even combining cookies and kooky predictions.

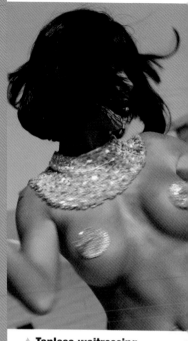

▲ Topless waitressing

At North Beach's Condor Club, waitress Carol "44 inches" Doda rolled down her top one day in 1964, and so ensured herself bigger tips and a place in history.

P.85 ▸ NORTH BEACH

▲ Cocoa butter

Gold miner-turned-grocer Domenico Ghirardelli discovered how to sweat the tasty butter out of raw cocoa – and made millions without panning a single nugget.

P.99 ▸ FISHERMAN'S WHARF AND ALCATRAZ

▲ Blue jeans

Levi Strauss came to the city planning to supply tents and wagon covers to Gold Rush miners, but ended up turning his tough fabric into work pants.

P.94 ▸ NOB HILL, RUSSIAN HILL AND TELEGRAPH HILL

▲ The martini

A triumphant Gold Rush miner is said to have asked for champagne and instead been served the bartender's "special" – a cocktail made from gin and vermouth he said was named after the town of Martinez.

P.75 ▸ UNION SQUARE AND AROUND

◀ Fortune cookies

Though Chinese-Americans in Los Angeles filed a rival claim to cooking up the idea, most people acknowledge Japanese Makota Hagiwara, who worked in the Japanese Tea Garden, as having created these as a token of thanks in 1907.

P.153 ▸ GOLDEN GATE PARK

◀ Chop Suey

Its exact origins are murky, but many claim that this dish – whose name derives from the Chinese character meaning "odds and ends" – was invented by Chinese-American laborers in San Francisco in the late nineteenth century.

P.82 ▸ CHINATOWN AND JACKSON SQUARE

Murals

Public art, often powered by protest, has long been welcomed in San Francisco; undoubtedly the local mural mastermind was Mexican transplant Diego Rivera. His thumpingly socialist artwork was the cause of much controversy back in the 1930s; today, it's revered rather than reviled, as evidenced by the many other modern murals that echo Rivera's style and concerns.

▲ Balmy Alley

This tiny alleyway's an ever-shifting gallery of protest art, as small murals are painted on wooden fences and replaced as soon as the colors fade.

P.132 ▸ THE MISSION

▲ Diego Rivera mural, SF Art Institute

A massive mural that exemplifies Rivera's art – from the socialist, worker-friendly theme to the contrariness of placing himself in the picture, albeit with his back to the viewer.

P.94 ▸ NOB HILL, RUSSIAN HILL AND TELEGRAPH HILL

▲ Diego Rivera murals, Coit Tower

The muscular murals around the base of this landmark are as artistically impressive today as they were when first painted in the 1930s, even if their communist sympathies are far less controversial.

P.92 ▶ NOB HILL, RUSSIAN HILL AND TELEGRAPH HILL

▲ Maxfield Parrish mural, Palace Hotel

Parrish's sprightly picture, painted especially for the hotel, shows a troupe of children entranced by the Pied Piper of Hamelin.

P.115 ▶ SOMA

▼ Defenestration outdoor wall sculpture

Local artist Brian Goggin created this piece of public art by bolting furniture to the exterior of an abandoned building.

P.116 ▶ SOMA

▲ Women's Building

Seven female designers plotted this massive mural, which tattoos the exterior of a community center, though it's more politically than artistically notable.

P.132 ▶ THE MISSION

Eccentric San Francisco

Outsiders, non-conformists and even the downright crazy have always found a welcome in San Francisco – famously nonjudgmental, this is a place where eccentrics have commandeered the mainstream. In the past, drag queens dressed as nuns have stood for city council and commune-dwelling hippies have staged free food giveaways to counteract the evils of capitalism; today, that same spirit still thrives in the city – here's the best of the wacky, weird and wonderful.

▲ Good Vibrations

Funky, friendly, and full of goodies, this store, run by a local collective, is a sex shop without shame.

P.133 ▶ THE MISSION

▲ Cliff's Variety

Castro mainstay, which sells a bizarre range of goods – pick up a feather boa as well as some hardware supplies. The friendly staff make it all the more neighborhoody.

P.140 ▶ THE CASTRO

▼ Bay to Breakers Race

The ultimate fancy dress party, in the guise of a race across town: look for the wags dressed as salmon who run backwards – or rather, "swim upstream."

P.202 › ESSENTIALS

▲ Amateur Opera Hour

The best time to come to *Caffe Trieste* is on Saturday afternoons during amateur opera hour, when karaoke sopranos fill the café with an irresistible (if offkey) choice of arias.

P.87 › NORTH BEACH

▶ Carol Doda's Champagne & Lace

Closet-sized lingerie store in a courtyard off the main drag in Cow Hollow, run by the world's first topless waitress.

P.109 › PACIFIC HEIGHTS AND THE NORTHERN WATERFRONT

Views of San Francisco

Official statistics put the number of hills within the city limits at a calf-aching 43, but the three closest to downtown – Telegraph, Nob and Russian – are the ones every visitor is likely to encounter and scale. Sadly, the views from these vantage points are often obscured by buildings, so we've picked out five fine alternatives if you want to snag a bird's-eye view of the city.

▲ Coit Tower

Perched on top of Telegraph Hill, this concrete tower looks back over the Financial District's forest of skyscrapers, as well as across the bay to Berkeley.

P.92 ▶ NOB HILL, RUSSIAN HILL AND TELEGRAPH HILL

▲ Campanile

On a cloudless day, you can see, beyond Berkeley's downtown, San Francisco bobbing on the horizon, its signature skyscrapers easily picked out against the sky.

P.168 ▶ BERKELEY

▶ Carnelian Room, Bank of America building

A rooftop cocktail lounge with gasp-inducing views across North Beach to Alcatraz – they're even better in the warm glow of dusk.

P.69 ▶ UNION SQUARE AND AROUND

▲ Alcatraz

Once you've finished exploring the deserted cells on "The Rock", walk down to the path which overlooks the city – on a clear day, there's a pristine view of downtown.

P.101 ▶ FISHERMAN'S WHARF AND ALCATRAZ

▼ Marin Headlands

Cycle, walk or drive across the Golden Gate Bridge to reach Marin, then swivel round to catch one of the best glimpses of the city's skyline.

P.177 ▶ THE WINE COUNTRY AND MARIN COUNTY

Literary San Francisco

Though their names may not all be familiar, each of the adoptive or locally-born San Franciscan writers we've cited here left a literary legacy for the city, whether Hamnett's hard-boiled detective fiction drawn from his own experiences or Jack London's folklore-inflected tales of wild Californian life.

▲ Jack Kerouac

The handsome, swaggering Kerouac became an icon of the beat movement with the publication of his novel On The Road; the time he spent in San Francisco is commemorated with a street name.

P.84 ▸ NORTH BEACH

▲ Ambrose Bierce

Known for its secretive camping retreats by corporate honchos, the *Bohemian Club* was originally an arty breakfast club that counted writers like Bierce among its number.

P.70 ▸ UNION SQUARE AND AROUND

▲ Dashiel Hammett

Several of Hammett's stories are set in the *Westin St Francis Hotel* – little wonder since his work as a private detective in the 1920s included the investigation of the rape and murder case against Fatty Arbuckle in the hotel.

P.69 ▸ UNION SQUARE AND AROUND

▼ Mark Twain

The satirist and Tom Sawyer creator spent plenty of time in the city usually at the Montgomery Block, a onetime lit hangout that's now the site of the famous pyramid-shaped Transamerica Building.

P.70 ▸ UNION SQUARE AND AROUND

▼ Jack London

The self-taught writer was born in Oakland and seemed destined to be an orphaned delinquent until his talent prevailed. He's beloved enough to snag an entire waterfront complex named in his honor.

P. 172 ▸ OAKLAND

Brunch

Don't wait till dinner to sample San Francisco's fabled food – breakfast and brunch is a prolonged gourmet affair here too. There are a few simple rules: bring a book (lines are always long and reservations rarely accepted), smile at the server (they're always harried), and always order the house special (it's guaranteed to be delicious).

▲ **Sears Fine Food**

A downtown diner, with frilly tablecloths and friendly service, that makes a welcome change from the tourist traps nearby.

P.74 ▸ UNION SQUARE AND AROUND

▲ Mama's

On weekends, the wait can be knee-achingly long, but it's certain to be worth it: there isn't a misstep on the marvelous menu.

`P.88` ▸ NORTH BEACH

▼ Ti Couz

This leisurely crêperie offers traditional buckwheat Breton pancakes with savory fillings as well as lighter, sweet versions like crêpes suzette with orange liqueur.

`P.135` ▸ THE MISSION

▲ Boogaloo's

This brightly colored diner serves Latin-inflected American brunch staples and showcases a rotating gallery of art on sale to raise money for disabled adults.

`P.133` ▸ THE MISSION

Places

Union Square and around

Three distinct neighborhoods form the core of San Francisco's downtown. Each is stitched along the northern edge of Market Street, which runs at a 45-degree angle through the heart of the city, binding the warehouse districts to the south with the chic shops and sleek offices immediately north. The most visited of these three neighborhoods is the shopping mecca of Union Square, which is fringed with upscale designer and department stores, not to mention hordes of hotels to house the credit-card-happy tourists. Immediately west stands the quieter and less commercial Theater District, its streets packed with old theaters, more hotels, and private clubs. Meanwhile, the land wedged between the San Francisco Bay and the eastern edge of Union Square is the canyon of skyscrapers known as the Financial District. It's mostly deserted at nights and on weekends but is home to San Francisco's signature building, the Transamerica Pyramid.

Union Square

Named after the Unionists who gathered to rally here on the eve of the Civil War, this square festered in recent years as a camping ground for the homeless but is now sparkling after a 2003 facelift. The center is stepped and paved, dotted with potted plants like a cozy patio, its edges marked with stout, pineapple-like palm trees.

▼ MACY'S DEPARTMENT STORE IN UNION SQUARE

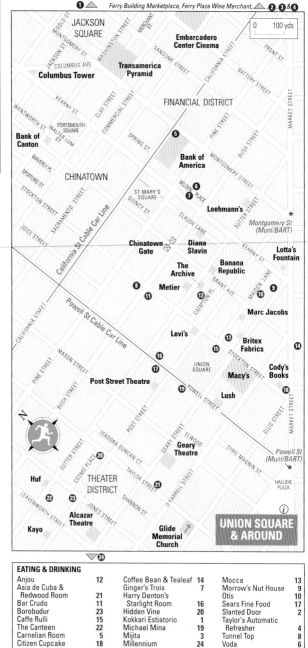

EATING & DRINKING

Anjou	12	Coffee Bean & Tealeaf	14	Mocca	13
Asia de Cuba &		Ginger's Trois	7	Morrow's Nut House	9
Redwood Room	21	Harry Denton's		Otis	10
Bar Crudo	11	Starlight Room	16	Sears Fine Food	17
Borobudur	23	Hidden Vine	20	Slanted Door	2
Caffe Rulli	15	Kokkari Estiatorio	1	Taylor's Automatic	
The Canteen	22	Michael Mina	19	Refresher	4
Carnelian Room	5	Mijita	3	Tunnel Top	8
Citizen Cupcake	18	Millennium	24	Voda	6

There's a handy café (*Caffè Rulli*) on the eastern edge, and ample seating – ideal for a break after browsing the dozens of shops that rim the square. This neighborhood's known for its shopping, especially the massive *Macy's* department store that fills

▲ CHIC BOUTIQUE ON MAIDEN LANE

the entire block south of the square. There are two local landmarks on the square itself: the Corinthian column at its center commemorates a victory in the Spanish-American War but is more notable for the woman, Alma de Bretteville, who scandalously posed for the scantily clad statue on its summit. De Bretteville was a wayward beauty who married sugar magnate Adolph Spreckels and then used his money to found the fantastic Legion of Honor art museum (see p.158) in the Richmond District. The other landmark is the opulent *Westin St Francis Hotel* (see p.189) on the square's western edge.

Maiden Lane

Dedicated designer label lovers should head to the north end of Union Square, where they'll find Maiden Lane, a small alleyway that was once a haven for hookers (hence the name) but is now known for its chic boutiques and upscale outdoor cafés.

Hallidie Plaza

Hallidie Plaza, at Powell and Market streets, is the one place in San Francisco through which just about every tourist will pass. The main San Francisco Visitor Information Center is here (see Essentials, p.197), overlooking a major Muni/BART train station; the plaza is also the terminus for the two cable car lines that run to the northern waterfront. The cable car was invented in 1873 by the plaza's namesake, Andrew Hallidie, an enterprising engineer who saw that San Francisco's hilly terrain would be better served by a mechanical alternative to horse-drawn carriages.

The Theater District

This neighborhood, sandwiched between gleaming Union Square and the grubby Tenderloin

▼ HALLIDIE PLAZA

▲ THE TRANSAMERICA PYRAMID

District is filled with hotels and old theaters. One of the most prominent theaters here is the Geary, a magnificent 1910 Beaux Arts building that was severely damaged in the 1989 earthquake, then reopened six years later after a massive retrofit, and now home to the American Conservatory Theater. The other impressive facade belongs to the now-derelict Alcazar Theatre (650 Geary St at Leavenworth), which is a former Masonic Temple originally designed to resemble an Islamic mosque. Showy as these theaters are, the blocks of Post and Sutter streets that cut through this area are home to some of downtown's least visible landmarks: about fourteen private clubs, which draw their members from San Francisco's society elite and whose existence is evidenced only by discreet and sometimes enigmatic metal plaques (the Bohemian Club's sign bears the motto "Weaving Spider Come Not Here").

Bank of America Building

555 California St at Kearny
ⓦ www.bankofamerica.com. The headquarters of California's largest financial institution, this enormous building was quite unpopular when finished in 1971; that's because its dark red granite facade offended architectural tastemakers, who wanted to preserve San Francisco's reputation as "a city of white." Affection's grown over the years for the broad-shouldered hulk, thanks to the stunning views from the *Carnelian Room* bar on its top floor (see p.75) as well as its starring role as the towering portion of campy 70s disaster classic *The Towering Inferno*.

The Transamerica Pyramid

600 Montgomery St at Clay
☏ 415/983-4100, ⓦ www.tapyramid .com. One of the city's signature sights, the Transamerica Pyramid is a glossy Financial District landmark designed by LA-based architect William Pereira in 1972. Nicknamed "Pereira's Prick," thanks to its tapering, priapic shape, this once controversial structure looks more like a squared-off rocket than a pyramid. The building's filled with nondescript offices and sadly, there's no longer public access to the viewing platform on the 27th floor. This skyscraper also occupies the site of the celebrated **Montgomery Block**, a four-story building that was home away from home for the city's literati, including Robert Louis Stevenson and Mark Twain, in the nineteenth century. It was unfortunately torn down to make way for a parking lot in 1959, though there's a commemorative brass plaque in the lobby.

The Embarcadero

Thanks to the traffic-clogged double-decker freeway that used

to loom over the waterfront (torn down in 1992 after being fatally damaged by the 1989 earthquake), the Embarcadero was for years a no-go area. But once the freeway was gone, this area – essentially the waterfront a few hundreds yards north and south of Market Street –became a magnet for hotels and restaurants taking advantage of the magnificent views across the bay. Today, the blocks just inland from the waterfront, bordering the Financial District are still dominated by the **Embarcadero Center** (www .embarcaderocenter.com). These four massive skyscrapers were built in the freeway days, and tall enough to snare views over the road out onto the bay; there's a bland mall that sprawls around their base. At the east end of this shopping hub sits the ugly modernist spectacle of **Vaillancourt Fountain**, which, on the last Friday of each month, is the meeting place for Critical Mass, when cyclists gather to promote bicycling as an environmentally friendly alternative to driving. At time of writing, the city had begun a major renovation plan intended to spruce up the Embarcadero's bleak edges to the south and enliven the piers north of here with new restaurants and museums. Bear in mind, though, it's likely to be a decade-long project.

Ferry Building

Junction of Market Street and Embarcadero ⓦwww.ferrybuilding-marketplace.com. Once the transit hub linking San Francisco with the East Bay, the Ferry Building, at the foot of Market Street, just underwent a stunning transformation into a gourmet mall, and is now packed with

▲ THE EMBARCADERO CENTER

wine merchants, artisanal cheese and chocolate shops as well as standout restaurants (see box). The best time to stop by is during the Ferry Plaza Farmers' Market (year-round Sat 8.30am–1.30pm, Tues & Sun 10am–2pm, also April–Nov Thurs 4–8pm; ☏415/291-3276, ⓦwww .ferryplazafarmersmarket.com), where local produce is sold from stalls set up in a skirt around the building. Local foodies make pilgrimages here to sample snacks from the city's pricy restaurants, which often set up temporary shacks among the fruit and vegetables – unbeatable for a picnic lunch.

Shops

The Archive

317 Sutter St at Grant Ave ☏415/391-5550, ⓦwww.archivesf.com. Superb, high-end menswear store run by the former Versace honcho in town, packed with obscure labels like Japanese conceptualist Kiminori Morishita.

Banana Republic

256 Grant Ave at Sutter ☏415/788-3087. The vast flagship branch of this national chain is especially noteworthy for its location, the

▲ VAILLANCOURT FOUNTAIN

White House, a historic five-story mansion whose interior has simply been whitewashed and preserved to form an impressive, cavernous backdrop to the casual clothes on sale.

Britex Fabrics

146 Geary St at Stockton ☎415/392-2910, ⓦwww.britexfabrics.com. A local institution, selling fabric and trims, as well as more than 30,000 kinds of buttons.

Cody's Books

2 Stockton St at Market ☎415/773-0444, ⓦwww.codysbooks.com. Brand-new megabranch of the East Bay's beloved bookstore, especially worthwhile for its twice-weekly author readings.

Diana Slavin

3 Claude Lane ☎415/677-9939 ⓦwww.dianaslavin.com. Closed Sun & Mon. Local designer Slavin's line of Calvin Klein–esque clothes for the chic career woman is available in this closet-sized store.

Huf

808 & 816 Sutter St at Jones ☎415/614-9414, ⓦwww.hufsf.com. Superb menswear store stocking skate and graffiti footwear and clothing with a stylish edge: think limited-edition Vans and retro decal tees, plus niche magazines, books, and a few skateboards.

Kayo

814 Post St at Leavenworth ☎415/749-0554, ⓦwww.kayobooks .com. Closed Mon & Tues. Glorious vintage paperback bookstore, crammed with bargain classics that include pulpy mysteries, sci-fi, and campy 1950s sleaze fiction.

Levi's

300 Post St at Stockton ☎415/501-0100. Four levels of jeans, tops, and jackets set amongst a thumping backdrop of club music. This flagship store stocks the entire Levi's line; it also offers the "Original Spin" service, where you can order customized denim.

Loehmann's

222 Sutter St at Kearny ☎415/982-3215. Root around for terrific designer bargains at this upscale discounter that's often crammed with same-season finds from the likes of DKNY and BCBG.

Marc Jacobs

125 Maiden Lane ☎415/362-6500. The patron saint of boho chic, Jacobs offers forties-inspired shoes

Ferry Building Marketplace

A superb new gourmet hub, the **Ferry Building Marketplace** has dozens of places to try, but there are a few true standouts, including:

Ferry Plaza Wine Merchant

☎415/391-9400, ⊛www.fpwm.com. You can sample one of the many available intriguing vintages before you buy, all for around $7 a glass, in their twenty-seater Taster Bar here. There are selections from California as well as lesser-known German, French, and Italian vineyards.

Mijita

☎415/399-0814, ⊛www.mijtasf.com. Chef Traci des Jardins took a break from five-star meals to open this excellent Mexican take-out, serving charred nuggets of pork piled high on a taco or a zesty jicama, grapefruit, and avocado salad for just $4.

Slanted Door

☎415/861-8032, ⊛www.slanteddoor.com. Gourmet French-Vietnamese restaurant with spectacular bay views and a sumptuous menu: don't miss the fiery green papaya salad that crackles with fried tofu and roasted peanuts. Lunchtime entrées cost $12–14, while at dinner the range is $15.50–26.50. At busy times, grab a stool at the bar or pick up takeout at the to-go window next door.

Taylor's Automatic Refresher

1-866/EAT-FOOD, ⊛www.taylorsrefresher.com. Upscale answer to a 1950s diner, serving everything from mahimahi fish and chips ($12.99) to burgers ($6.99–8.99). Grab a bench outdoors and feast on a bacon, blue cheese, and BBQ burger, washed down with a gloopy white pistachio milkshake ($4.50).

and colorful, thrift-store-like threads, albeit at designer prices.

Metier

355 Sutter St at Grant Ave ☎415/989-5395, ⊛www.metiersf.com. A gallery of girly, up-and-coming clothing labels, like Mayle and Language. There's also high-end hipster wear from Development and antique-inspired jewelry by Cathy Waterman.

Cafés and snacks

Bar Crudo

603 Bush St at Stockton ☎415/956-0396. Swanky cupboard-sized eatery serving superb fish snacks like prawn calamari and artichoke salad ($11) or scallops ($10). Order a glass of wine and snuggle in at a table in the loft, or snag a bar stool on the first floor.

Caffè Rulli

Stockton Street Pavilion, 333 Post St ☎415/433-1122. Café on Union Square's plaza that serves bracingly strong coffee and Italian pastries. There are tables outside if you want to lounge.

The Canteen

inside the Commodore Hotel, 817 Sutter St at Jones ☎415/928-8870. Hidden in the hotel, this upscale diner is a standout for its homey food, like pork chops and steak tartare for around $12 a head; don't miss the homemade ginger ale.

Citizen Cupcake

inside the Virgin Megastore, 3rd floor, 2 Stockton St at Market ☎415/399-1565, ⓦwww.citizencake.com. Tasty café stashed inside the record megaplex with coffee, tea, sake, and Asian-inflected sandwiches/salads as well as the namesake cupcakes.

Coffee Bean and Tea Leaf

773 Market St at 4th ☎415/896-5029, ⓦwww.coffeebean.com. Newbie outpost of the terrific Angeleno answer to Starbucks: order one of the signature Iced Blendeds and settle in at a table out front on the sidewalk.

Mocca

175 Maiden Lane ☎415/956-1188. Small Italian café with plenty of outdoor seating; for around $7, sample a Mediterranean sandwich packed with tasty cured meats and pickles.

Morrow's Nut House

111 Geary St at Grant ☎415/362-7969. Tiny store selling nuts, candies and dried fruits by the piece or the pound – grab a healthy snack like Oregon dry-roasted filberts or Mexican pumpkin seeds to go.

Sears Fine Food

439 Powell St at Post ☎415/986-1160. New owners have remade this Union Square legend into an all-day bistro, so while it's still a top-notch breakfast joint (the 18 tiny Swedish pancakes, served all day, cost $7.95), there is now a dinner menu of pasta and salads.

Restaurants

Anjou

44 Campton Place at Stockton ☎415/392-5373. This French bistro on a quiet side street near the square, is great for a bargain-priced prix fixe lunch: soup or salad, plus an entrée like an ahi tuna sandwich or crab parmentier, for $16.

Asia de Cuba

inside the Clift Hotel, 495 Geary St at Taylor ☎415/923-2300. Sino-Cuban fusion food in a funky setting, combining the freshness of Chinese cooking with the plentifulness of Cuban cuisine. The food's served family-style in huge portions and delivered dish by dish as soon as it's ready: try the tuna tartare on wonton crisps. Pricey (expect to spend at least $80 a head) but a treat, nonetheless.

Borobudur

700 Post St at Jones ☎415/775-1512, ⓦwww.borobudursf.com. Smallish Indonesian restaurant's hick curries, which mix Indian and Thai influences, are particularly good, and a full dinner shouldn't cost more than $15. Come early to avoid the karaoke.

Kokkari Estiatorio

200 Jackson St at Front ☎415/981-0983, ⓦwww.kokkari.com. By far the best Greek restaurant in town (and the priciest – budget $40 a head), serving plenty of eggplant and lamb, as well as a killer yogurt sorbet.

Michael Mina

inside the Westin St. Francis Hotel, 335 Powell St at Post ☎415/397-9222, ⓦwww.michaelmina.net. Dinner only. Take out a mortgage, postpone the diet, and dust off that suit if you want to enjoy the extraordinary food at this five-star standout: there's an $88 three-course prix fixe menu with options like potato-crusted John Dory or six-hour butter-poached prime rib.

Millennium

inside the *Savoy Hotel*, 580 Geary St at Hyde ☎415/345-3900, ⊛www.millenniumrestaurant.com. Legendary vegetarian restaurant, offering flavor-packed entrees ($20–22), like fried portobello mushrooms, robust enough to please even avid meat eaters. The dark wood-paneled decor's gauzy and romantic, and the crowd's as much opera buff as eco-warrior.

Bars

Carnelian Room

555 California St at Montgomery ☎415/431-7500, ⊛www.carnelianroom.com. Fifty-two floors up in the Bank of America Building, this elegant rooftop cocktail lounge has fantastic views of North Beach, Alcatraz, and the Transamerica Pyramid, especially at sunset. It's reached by an express elevator from the basement of the skyscraper.

Ginger's Trois

246 Kearny St at Bush ☎415/989-0282. A charming, low-rent gay bar smack in the heart of downtown; the bartenders sometimes play sing-along show tunes on the piano.

Harry Denton's Starlight Room

inside the *Sir Francis Drake Hotel*, 450 Powell St at Sutter ☎415/395-8595, ⊛www.harrydenton.com. Dress up and drink martinis while swaying to live music from the Starlight Orchestra at this famous watering hole.

Hidden Vine

620 Post St at Taylor ☎415/674-3567. Sneak into this intimate and warm, speakeasy-style wine bar and sink into one of the comfy armchairs with a glass or two of California wine.

Otis

25 Maiden Lane ☎No public phone, ⊛www.otissf.com. Private club-style bar (nonmembers can sup from 2 to 9pm) that looks like a jet-setting porn star's living room from the 1970s. Expect a snooty but trendy crowd with a distinctly New York edge.

The Redwood Room

inside the *Clift Hotel*, 495 Geary St at Taylor ☎415/775-4700. Clubby landmark drinking hole that was recently given a postmodern makeover by Philippe Starck: the freakish light boxes on the wall display paintings that shift and fade – pity the drink prices are so outrageous.

Tunnel Top

601 Bush St at Stockton ☎415/986-8900. Funky dive bar on top of the Stockton Street Tunnel that's been recently done over and is now a bit swankier, complete with cocktails made from fresh juices.

Voda

56 Belden Place at Bush ☎415/677-9242, ⊛www.vodasf.com. Design-conscious bar with a gimmick of a 100-plus list of vodkas; its appeal is the moody vibe, dressy crowd, and the outdoor banquettes where you can sip a cocktail on a summer evening.

Performing arts and film

American Conservatory Theater (ACT)

Geary Theater, 415 Geary St at Taylor ☎415/742-2228,

ⓦwww.act-sfbay.org. This is the Bay Area's leading resident theater group, known for its inventive staging (recent seasons have included *Waiting for Godot* and *Les Liaisons Dangereuses*). Tickets start at around $20.

Embarcadero Center Cinema

1 Embarcadero Center at Sansome ☎415/267-4893. ⓦwww .landmarktheatres.com. Beautifully situated close to the water's edge, this is the only art-house multiplex downtown, showing offbeat indies and Oscar-chasing dramas.

Post Street Theatre

450 Post St at Powell ☎415/433-9500, ⓦwww.450poststreet.com. Converted neo-Gothic theater, mostly housing mainstream crowd-pleasers – whether musicals like the recent hit 25th Annual Putnam County Spelling Bee or Neil Simon–style stage sitcoms and dramas. Tickets from $50.

Chinatown and Jackson Square

San Francisco, with its throbbing, noisy Chinatown, is home to the second-largest Chinese community outside Asia (only New York City bests it). The neighborhood has its roots in the mostly Cantonese laborers who migrated there after the completion of the transcontinental railroad. A rip-roaring prostitution and gambling quarter (controlled by gangs, or tongs) developed during the nineteenth century but faded after World War II. The energy and crowds remain today, but it's touristy as rather than seedy as people come to sample dim sum at one of the dozens of restaurants or buy a cheap souvenir from one of the throngs of nearly identical shops. Nearby Jackson Square is a studied contrast, a flash-frozen glimpse of nineteenth-century San Francisco, ghostly and evocative and now mostly home to upscale interior designers' showrooms.

Grant Avenue

Grant Avenue is Chinatown's main north-south artery, lined with gold-ornamented portals, brightly painted balconies, and some of the tackiest stores and facades in the city. One of San Francisco's oldest thoroughfares, it was originally known as DuPont Street, and its wicked ensemble of opium dens, bordellos, and gambling huts was policed – if not terrorized – by *tong* hatchet men. The road was renamed in honor of Civil War hero Ulysses S. Grant after the 1906 fire.

▼ CHINATOWN GATE

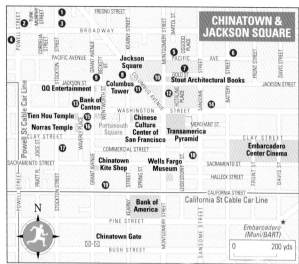

CHINATOWN & JACKSON SQUARE

EATING & DRINKING

Bix	7	Great Eastern	11	Lichee Garden	2	Sam Who	16
Bubble Lounge	12	Hang Ah Tea Room	17	Lucky Creation	13	Scott Howard	10
Buddha Bar	15	House of Nanking	8	Il Massimo del Panino	14	Tlaloc	18
Cathay House	19	Imperial Tea Court	4	Mee Mee Bakery	1	Yuet Lee	3
The Globe	6	Li Po's Bar	9	Myth	5		

The gate that caps the avenue on the south end at Bush Street was a gift from the People's Republic of China to the city in 1969. It faces south, per feng shui precepts, and the four-character inscription reads *Xia tian wei gong*, or "The reason to exist is to serve the public good."

Grant is at its least tourist-tacky on the stretch just south of Columbus; but to best sample everyday life in Chinatown, head to souvenir-stall-free Stockton Street, the commercial strip where most locals shop for groceries.

Waverly Place

This tiny backstreet was once the heart of Chinatown's extensive network of brothels but is now known for a couple of opulent but out-of-sight temples. The namesake deity of Norras temple (third floor, no. 149) was the first lama from Tibet to teach high-level Buddhism in China; the chatty custodians will happily share stories. Meanwhile, Tien Hou (pronounced TEE-en How) temple (fourth floor, no. 125) commemorates the Taoist Goddess of Heaven; this is a more formal affair than the Norras temple, with gaudier decor and a ceiling dripping with red tasseled lanterns. Note the tiny mirrors fastened to the balcony of 829 Sacramento Street, at the eastern end of Waverly Place: they're designed to ward off evil spirits.

Portsmouth Square

Washington St and Grant Ave.
Though it's now an outpost of Chinatown, filled with

▲ STOCKTON STREET

temple-like structures and older Chinese locals practicing tai chi or playing rowdy games of chess, Portsmouth Square is in fact the site of the oldest European settlement in San Francisco. An English adventurer named William Richardson petitioned the Mexican government in 1835 for permission to establish a trading post here, which he called Yerba Buena after the sweet, mint-like plant that local Native Americans stewed into tea. Eleven years later, when American sailors came ashore to claim the colony for the United States, they raised their flag in the small square at the center of Richardson's hamlet – look for the pennant flying today that marks the spot.

The best time to come here is on Saturday evening from spring through autumn (6–11pm), when a night market animates the square with performances of classical opera and traditional music surrounded by stalls selling everything from fresh honey to leather jackets; undeniably hokey, but lively fun.

Bank of Canton

743 Washington St at Grant Ave ☎415/421-5215. This small, red, pagoda-inspired building was constructed in 1909 to house the Chinese-American Telephone Exchange: note how the roof curves out and then back on itself to foil evil spirits (they can only travel in a straight line, apparently). This was also the site of the offices of the *California Star* newspaper, which carried the news of the earliest

▼ BANK OF CANTON

▲ HANGING DUCKS FOR SALE

ore discoveries back to the East Coast in 1848 and so breathlessly hyped the Gold Rush.

Chinese Culture Center of San Francisco

inside the *Hilton Hotel*, 3rd floor, 750 Kearny St at Washington, ☏415/986-1822, ⓦwww.c-c-c.org. Easily missed, tucked inside the Hilton Hotel, this intriguing center has free exhibits on different aspects of Chinese culture four times yearly, as well as classes in everything from tai chi and Mandarin to calligraphy and brush painting (sign up for a single session for $15). It also runs walking tours of the area ($40 including lunch). Be forewarned, however, the staff at the front desk are often grumpy and unwelcoming.

Jackson Square

bordered by Washington and Sansome streets and Pacific and Columbus avenues. The Jackson Square Historic District, a cluster of Victorian buildings that survived the 1906 earthquake and fire, is a charming anomaly. But despite their

obvious architectural appeal, the restored red-brick houses here were spared from the blaze for prosaic rather than poetic reasons: the area was doused in water to ensure that 5000 barrels of highly flammable whiskey (stashed in the Hotaling Building, 451–455 Jackson St) didn't catch fire. It's not surprising that whiskey was stored in such large amounts here: Jackson Square, then known as the Barbary Coast, was San Francisco's answer to New York's Five Points: a decadent district full of brothels, bars, and vaudeville houses. These days little evidence remains of the district's sordid history. The winding brickwork, hitching posts, and antique lamps of Hotaling Place, running for a block south from Jackson Street, are an evocative time capsule of nineteenth-century San Francisco; but while it's a fine enough place to stroll around today, there are few places to browse other than upscale interior-design studios.

Shops

Chinatown Kite Shop

717 Grant Ave at Sacramento ☏415/ 989-5182, ⓦwww .chinatownkite.com. You can buy cheap, throwaway kitschy kites or investment-grade professional flyers, plus a smattering of Chinatown souvenirs, at this longtime local landmark.

Ellison Herb Shop

801-805 Stockton St at Sacramento. Daily 11am–7pm. Double-fronted store: one section's tacky souvenirs, but the more interesting side is the herbal pharmacy, where you'll still find clerks filling orders the ancient

Chinese way – with handheld scales and abaci – from drug cabinets filled with dried bark, shark fins, cicadas, ginseng, and other staples.

QQ Entertainment

956 Grant Ave at Jackson ☎ 415/398-5068. Media HQ packed with Chinese-language music and movies on DVD, VHS, and CD. Canto-pop heaven.

Stout Architectural Books

804 Montgomery St at Jackson ☎ 415/391-6757, ⓦ www.stoutbooks.com. One of San Francisco's world-class booksellers, with an excellent range of books on architecture, building, and urban studies.

Cafés and snacks

Hang Ah Tea Room

1 Pagoda Place, off Sacramento St at Stockton ☎ 415/982-5686. Fri & Sat until 1am. Tasty neighborhood dim sum eatery with two major pluses – it's open late and prices are low ($5 for a rice plate, $2 or so for dim sum).

Il Massimo del Panino

441 Washington St at Sansome ☎ 415/834-0290. Unsurprisingly, given that it's next door to the Instituto Italiano di Cultura, this panini shop serves authentic pressed sandwiches and salads – fortunately, they're delicious, as well.

Imperial Tea Court

1411 Powell St at Broadway ☎ 415/788-6080. Steep yourself in the ambience of an old-world teahouse worthy of the last emperor: a peaceful bolt-hole amid the craziness of Chinatown.

Of the 32 varieties on offer, try the Jade Fire blend tea.

Lichee Garden

1416 Powell St at Broadway ☎ 415/397-2290. Classy dim sum served daily 7am–3pm at this restaurant filled with potted plants and carved wall hangings; if you opt for larger Cantonese dishes instead of dim sum, entrées cost $6-8.

Mee Mee Bakery

1328 Stockton St at Broadway ☎ 415/362-3204. Little-known gem that serves delicate almondy treats as well as a variety of fortune cookies: plain ones cost $2.60 per half pound, special flavors and fortunes (biblical, adult) a buck more.

Tlaloc

525 Commercial St at Sansome ☎ 415/981-7800. Tasty, cheap, modern Mexican ideal for a quick lunch on the go: eat in or take out specials like a chicken mole burrito ($8.75) or breakfast plates like chorizo con huevos ($5.50). Breakfast and lunch only.

Restaurants

Bix

56 Gold St at Montgomery ☎ 415/433-6300, ⓦ www.bixrestaurant.com. Named after 1930s jazz cornetist Bix Beiderbecke, this high-end supper club on a red brick side street has live music every night and no cover. The food's modern American, but it's the martinis and retro ambience that are the real draws.

The Globe

290 Pacific Ave at Battery ☎ 415/391-4132. The best place to grab

▲ LEMON CHICKEN SOUP IN CHINATOWN

dinner after hours alongside the waiters who flock here once their shift's ended – dinner's served until 1am and includes meat and fish entrées like grilled *bistecca* or shrimp baked in a wood oven (most cost $18–21).

Great Eastern

649 Jackson St at Kearny ☎415/986-2500. Located behind an impressive pagoda facade, this rather elegant, traditional Chinese restaurant specializes in seafood dishes like an excellent turtle soup. Prices are swankier than those of many of the other nearby restaurants (entrées around $15), but then again, so's the decor. On a warm day, try to get a spot on the outdoor balcony.

House of Nanking

919 Kearny St at Jackson ☎415/421-1429. Tiny, legendary restaurant – expect a long line (which will move faster than you expect) – grumpy service, and a fabulous, underpriced meal of Chinese standards like Shanghai dumplings ($5.95).

Lucky Creation

854 Washington St at Waverly ☎415/989-0818. Budget vegan option, with imaginative faux-meat dishes created from tofu and wheat gluten that's been chopped and shaped so that it can even look like a cutlet or wing. Try the sautéed straw mushrooms with snow peas ($4.95) or deep-fried crispy taro rolls ($5.90).

Myth

470 Pacific Ave at Montgomery ☎415/677-8986. One of the hottest tables in town, Myth's modernist design features cozy wooden cubbyholes for banquettes. The chef creates tasty riffs on California classics: try the prawn cocktail pizza with pancetta. Entrées cost around $20–28.

Sam Wo

813 Washington St at Grant ☎415/982-0596. Mon–Sat until 3am. Popular late-night spot where Kerouac, Ginsberg, and others used to hold court – expect very cheap but mediocre food,

brusque service, and lashings of atmosphere.

Scott Howard

500 Jackson St at Montgomery ☏415/956-7040, ⊛www .scotthowardsf.com. Enormous, Cal-French eatery with a low-key Pottery Barn look but high-end food: dinner mains run $21-28 and range from poussin with heart of palm to sturgeon with veal cheeks. The asparagus and Meyer lemon risotto's a delicious appetizer ($10).

Yuet Lee

1300 Stockton St at Broadway ☏415/982-6020. Daily until 3am. Easily spotted thanks to its garish green exterior, this pricey diner has on-site fish tanks, so you know the seafood is fresh – try steamed fish or clams with black bean sauce for around $10 a dish or if you're brave, a bowl of steamed frogs ($18).

Bars

Bubble Lounge

714 Montgomery St at Columbus ☏415/434-4204 ⊛www .bubblelounge.com. Closed Sun. Champagne bar that attracts a young, gussied- and Gucci'd-up crowd with its surprisingly reasonable prices.

Buddha Bar

901 Grant Ave at Washington ☏415/362-1792. Darkish bar decorated with twinkling fairy lights that feels far removed from urban America, filled with older locals slapping down mah-jongg tiles.

Cathay House

718 California St at Grant ☏415/982-3388. There's an inviting circular bar at the center of this so-so restaurant, presided over by a massive statue of the Buddha.

Li Po's Bar

916 Grant Ave at Jackson ☏415/982-0072. Named after the Chinese poet, this raucous and kitschy bar is something of a literary hangout among Chinatown regulars: try and bag one of the red booths at the back. Inexplicably, there's also a photo booth inside for drunken quick snaps.

North Beach

Inland North Beach is a sunny neighborhood sitting in a valley sheltered by several hills, and is known as the hub of San Francisco's Italian community (for the record, the area was named while still on the waterfront, before landfill extended the peninsula). The freewheeling European atmosphere here made the area attractive to 1950s Beat writers, who helped turn San Francisco into a beacon for later counterculturalists like the hippies and flower children. Today, though the Beats are long gone and North Beach is thoroughly gentrified, it still retains a pungent enough Italian flavor to draw hungry or nostalgic tourists to walk its streets or hang out in one of the legendary cafés – and any espresso served here puts Starbucks to shame. Most of the sights and facilities jostle together along Columbus Avenue, the main drag that marks the boundary between North Beach here and Chinatown and Russian Hill to the west.

City Lights Bookstore

261 Columbus Ave at Broadway ☎415/362-8193, ⓦwww.citylights .com. An independent bookstore that was the heart of Beat North Beach, City Lights still fights on today under original owner Lawrence Ferlinghetti, now well into his eighties. Ferlinghetti was an early advocate and publisher of the Beats, the loose writers' collective that included Jack Kerouac and Allen Ginsberg and whose bohemian lifestyle was the *succès de scandale* of the 1950s. The best reason to stop by City Lights – aside from experiencing its astonishingly grumpy staff firsthand – is the upstairs poetry room, well

▼ NORTH BEACH RESIDENTS HANGING OUT AT AN ITALIAN CAFÉ

NORTH BEACH

EATING & DRINKING		Fior d'Italia	1	Jazz at Pearl's	22	Panelli's	12
Bimbo's 365 Club	2	Gino and Carlo	10	L'Osteria del Forno	7	Rosewood	16
Café Jacqueline	8	The Helmand	18	Liguria Bakery &		Savoy Tivoli	9
Caffè Greco	14	Il Pollaio	11	Mama's	3	Spec's Adler	
Caffè Macaroni	24	Iluna Basque	5	Mario's Bohemian		Museum Café	23
Caffè Trieste	19	Impala	17	Cigar Store	6	The Velvet Lounge	20
Citizen Thai &		Italian French		Mojito	13	Vesuvio	21
the Monkey	15	Bakery	4				

stocked with not only Beat masterworks but also lesser-known modern verse.

Andrew Jaeger at the Condor Club

300 Columbus Ave at Broadway
☎415/781-8222, ⓦwww.condorsf
.com. Though now, bizarrely, a tacky, New Orleans-reffing Creole eatery, this spot was once the site of the notorious Condor Club, where in 1964, server Carol "44 inches" Doda (see box, p.86) slipped out of her top and into the history books by becoming the first-ever topless waitress.

Washington Square Park

This grassy plaza with ample benches is the soul of North Beach, serving as a playground for local children as well as a workout studio for older Chinese locals, who appear each morning in scattered groups and silently practice tai chi. The beefy bronze statue on its western edge was donated by Lillie Coit, a wealthy but wacky woman who was obsessed with firemen. In their honor, she donated

▼ CITY LIGHTS BOOKSTORE

▲ PRACTICING TAI CHI NEAR THE CHURCH OF SAINTS PETER AND PAUL

lacy spires of this church look like a pair of picturesque fairy-tale castle towers. Although it's seen as the spiritual home of the local Italian community, the church also now offers Mass in Cantonese, as well as Italian and English, reflecting the shifting character of the neighborhood.

money for two memorials: her massive, namesake tower on Telegraph Hill (apparently aping a fireman's hose) and the cluster of statues here depicting burly volunteer firefighters, one of whom carries a swooning maiden no doubt inspired by Lillie herself.

Church of Saints Peter and Paul

660 Filbert St at Columbus ☎415/421-5219, ⍓www.stspeterpaul.san-francisco.ca.us. The white

Shops

A. Cavaili & Co

1441 Stockton St at Columbus ☎415/421-4219. Italian-language bookstore with magazines, books, and movies.

alla prima

1420 Grant Ave at Green ☎415/397-4077. Upscale lingerie outlet: there's a wall of pricey but beautiful frilly bras, fresh flowers everywhere, and fancy sex toys.

Graffeo Coffee

733 Columbus Ave at Filbert ☎415/986-2420, ⍓www.graffeo.com. There are huge sacks of coffee piled up all over this store, where the Repetto family has been roasting coffee for more than sixty years.

Carol Doda

Carol "44 inches" Doda is an unsung pioneer of the Sexual Revolution. Knowing that she'd make bigger tips by baring her best assets, the North Beach cocktail waitress kick-started topless waitressing on June 19, 1964. But the idea wasn't as impromptu as legend has it – the bouncer and the club's owner together cooked up the plot to grab headlines and cash by as outrageous a gesture as laws allowed. They selected Carol, with her blonde ringlets and saucy manner, as the nipple-baring pioneer and publicized the stunt to locals and visiting politicians in town for the Republican Convention. Thanks to the controversy and Doda's own notoriety, business boomed and her fellow cocktail carriers started offering semi-clothed service, too. The final step came five years later, when the ever intrepid Carol, looking to grab headlines again, dropped trou completely and started nude waitressing. She went on to a long and lucrative career; these days, the ageless Doda may be retired, but she's a cult figure, who owns a lingerie emporium in the Marina (see p.109).

The Beats

The best-known **Beats** – Allen Ginsberg, William Burroughs, and Jack Kerouac – first met up in New York in the 1940s but, disillusioned, soon moved to North Beach and secured jobs at the docks to help longshoremen unload the fishing boats (the cheap rent and cheap red wine were other draws). When City Lights opened in 1953 here, as the first bookstore in America devoted to paperbacks, it was clear that the literary rumblings around town were growing louder. It wasn't until four years later, though, when Ginsberg's pornographic poem "Howl," a pervy protest piece that attracted media and police scrutiny, that the Beats surfaced in mainstream culture (Ginsberg's case went all the way to the Supreme Court, which eventually ruled in 1957 that so long as a work has "redeeming social value," it could not be considered pornographic).

Of course, the Beats shattered traditional literary rules in the way they wrote – Kerouac, a former speed-typing champion, created a personal style by hammering out his works free-form in emulation of the solos of jazz musicians. Just as important, though, they challenged traditional societal rules in the way they lived. Soon North Beach was synonymous across America with a wild, subversive lifestyle, though the crazy hedonism lasted only a few years before national attention (and outrage) shifted to the blissed-out hippies of the Haight-Ashbury (see p.146).

Molinari's

373 Columbus Ave at Vallejo ☎415/421-2337. North Beach deli/grocery jammed to the rafters with Italian goodies – buy a hunk of parmesan to take home.

Paparazzi

1424 Grant Avenue at Green ☎415/399-1118. Girly, Anthropologie-style boutique with clothes from Free People and Three Dot plus ethnic/vintage-styled homewares, throws, and cushions.

Cafés and snacks

Caffè Greco

423 Columbus Ave at Vallejo ☎415/397-6261. Pull up a plastic chair at one of the small marble tables and gaze at the faded Italian adverts on the wall; top-notch coffee, crunchy biscotti and especially friendly staff.

Caffe Trieste

601 Vallejo St at Grant ☎415/392-6739. Small, crowded Italian coffeehouse noted for its Saturday-afternoon amateur opera hour. Francis Ford Coppola is rumored to have scribbled out the script for *The Godfather* here.

▼ CAFFE TRIESTE

Italian French Bakery

1501 Grant Ave at Union ☎415/421-3796. The huge on-site ovens at the back of this tiny bakery waft the smell of fresh breads all along the block: tear into hearty focaccia as well as traditional pastries ($1.25–1.50).

Liguria Bakery

1700 Stockton St at Filbert ☎415/421-3786. Old-world Italian bakery selling fresh focaccia – get there by noon as it closes once they're sold out.

Mama's

1701 Stockton St at Washington Square ☎415/362-6421. Tues–Sun 8am–3pm. Hands-down one of the best brunches in the city – try the crab Benedict or a gooey serving of French toast. There are certain to be massive lines at the weekend, but it's well worth the wait.

Mario's Bohemian Cigar Store

566 Columbus Ave at Union ☎415/362-0536. No cigars anymore, but the café still serves good coffee and bulging, cheap sandwiches

(made with bread from the Liguria Bakery – see above).

Panelli's

1419 Stockton St at Columbus ☎415/421-2541. Old-school Italian sandwich shop serving enormous, meaty sandwiches for around $7 each.

Restaurants

Café Jacqueline

1454 Grant Ave at Green ☎415/981-5565. It's all soufflés, all the time at this romantic, candlelit restaurant with its classic white tablecloths and hushed atmosphere. The menu's crammed with fluffy savory and sweet concoctions - the strawberry soufflé is especially fresh and superb. Book ahead and save up – it's priced for celebration evenings.

Caffè Macaroni

59 Columbus Ave at Jackson ☎415/956-9737. Tiny, intimate date restaurant that serves well-made antipasti and main courses including buttery plates of gnocchi at close to budget prices – don't worry if the tiny,

▼ MARIO'S BOHEMIAN CIGAR STORE

street-side room looks too full, as there's extra seating upstairs.

Citizen Thai and the Monkey

1268 Grant Ave at Vallejo, ☏415/364-0008, ⊛www.citizenthai.com. Combo café and restaurant: hit the casual bar next door for noodle and rice dishes, plus street-food snacks and drinks, or settle for a full meal in the main dining room. Mains run $12–16; the brave should sample the *nahm prik* dipping sauce, Thailand's fiery answer to fondue ($12).

Fior d'Italia

in the *San Remo Hotel*, 2237 Mason St at Chestnut ☏415/986-1886, ⊛www.fior.com. Fior maintains a deliberately old-fashioned aura thanks to its bow-tied waiters (after all, it claims to be the oldest Italian restaurant in America). The menu's full of robust, rich pastas at reasonable prices (around $16).

The Helmand

430 Broadway at Kearny ☏415/362-0641. Originally owned by the brother of premier Hamid Karzai, the food at this Afghan eatery is unforgettable, filled with tangy and spicy Afghani staples: try the *kaddo borwani* (caramelized pumpkin on a bed of yoghurt).

Iluna Basque

701 Union St at Powell ☏415/402-0011 ⊛www.ilunabasque.com. Those who are new to Basque cuisine will appreciate this café's old country appeal: dark wood walls, red and black decor, and a huge bar full of robust red wines. The menu features tapas-sized treats plus occasional French touches like cassoulet ($8-10). There's an all-day coffee shop next door, Eguna Basque, that serves coffee and panini ($6.50).

L'Osteria del Forno

519 Columbus Ave at Green ☏415/982-1124. Gloriously authentic Italian gem that's one of the best restaurants in the area, with a small, market-driven menu – try the roast pork braised in milk if it's available – priced in a wallet-friendly fashion.

Mojito

1337 Grant Ave at Vallejo ☏415/398-1120. Weekdays dinner only, closed Mon. Always slammed, this hipster-friendly spot is best known for bringing the jazz brunch back to the 'hood. Whatever the time, expect a worthwhile wait for Latin specials like papas fritas ($5) or grilled sirloin with garlic prawns and cilantro ($16).

Il Pollaio

555 Columbus Ave at Union ☏415/362-7727. Chow down on killer rotisserie chicken at this bustling local spot, or take it to go. The moist, crispy skin pairs well with a grilled bean salad loaded with tangy vinaigrette.

Bars

Gino and Carlo

548 Green St at Grant ☏415/421-0896. Classic pub aimed at hardened barflies, open at 6am for night-shift workers on their way home and filled with old-school locals all day.

Impala

501 Broadway at Kearny ☏415/982-5299. Upscale Mexican spot with ranch-inspired decor and a trendy crowd: skip the restaurant and head instead for the smaller, cozy lounge downstairs. There's a DJ most nights, spinning house and hip-hop.

Rosewood

732 Broadway at Powell ☎415/951-4886. There's no sign outside this retro groovy bar, known for killer cocktails and loungecore DJs – avoid the weekends, unless you want to join the crush of out-of-towners on the sidewalk waiting to get in.

Savoy Tivoli

1434 Grant Ave at Green ☎415/361-7023. Sprawling North Beach institution (dating back to 1907) filled with a mix of old-timers and hipsters. There's a smoker-friendly open-air patio, a couple of pool tables – it feels like a boho beatnik hangout.

Spec's Adler Museum Café

12 Saroyan Place at Columbus ☎415/421-4112. Friendly dive bar in the heart of North Beach, where an older, eccentric local crowd hangs out with the chatty bar staff.

Vesuvio

255 Columbus Ave at Broadway ☎415/362-3370, ⓦwww.vesuvio.com. The interior of this famed Beat haunt looks like an explosion in a scrapbook factory – the walls are covered with collages and photos. It's friendly and low key, and despite its historic reputation there are equal numbers of tourists and locals propping up the bar.

Performing arts and film

Beach Blanket Babylon at Club Fugazi

678 Green St at Powell ☎415/421-4222, ⓦwww.beachblanketbabylon.com. Wed–Sun. Unmissable local theatrical institution, a lampooning revue based loosely on Snow White's quest to find a man like *Saturday Night Live* with better and bigger wigs. The quick-fire humor and charm of the mostly veteran performers guarantees a riotous evening – it doesn't hurt that drinks are served, either. Tickets $33–65; 21 and over only.

▼ VESUVIO

Clubs and live music

Bimbo's 365 Club

1025 Columbus at Chestnut
℡415/474-0365, ⓦwww.bimbos365
.com. This historic and traditional 1940s supper club offers more than just Frank Sinatra tribute bands, thanks to a savvy booker who also schedules underground European acts and big names like Coldplay and Zero 7. $20 and up.

Jazz at Pearl's

256 Columbus at Broadway
℡415/291-8255, ⓦwww.jazzatpearls
.com. Jazz vocalist Kim Nalley has revived this once moribund spot and schedules nightly sets by a rotating cast of regulars; she sings most Tuesdays. $5–15.

The Velvet Lounge

443 Broadway at Montgomery
℡415/788-0228, ⓦwww
.thevelvetlounge.com. About the only spot for the under-thirty set to dance in North Beach; the stage is often open to live rock bands. Weekends can be a meat market. $10.

Nob Hill, Russian Hill, and Telegraph Hill

These three hills are the highest points in the center of the city, so make sure to wear comfortable shoes while exploring. Telegraph Hill (named after an old communications station that once stood here) holds a quiet cluster of hill-hugging homes that cascade down to the waterfront on its eastern edge. Upscale Russian Hill (named after six unknown Russian sailors buried here in the early 1800s), with its leafy, tree-lined streets, is largely residential, the summit capped by a few modest high-rise apartment buildings; it's served by a chic strip of shops and cafés along upper Polk Street and most often visited for those looking to take a white-knuckle ride down twisty Lombard Street. And Nob Hill (whose moniker comes from the rich industrial "nabobs" who settled here in the late nineteenth century after the cable car made it residentially accessible) is the snootiest of all – hushed and wealthy, with few attractions other than its multimillion-dollar homes.

Coit Tower

☏ 415/362-0808, ⓦ www.coittower .org. Daily 10am–5pm. $3.75. Loopy local eccentric Lillie Coit was obsessed with firemen and spent her life hanging out at firemen's balls and playing poker with her firefighting buddies. On her death in 1929, Lillie left a chunk of her sizable fortune to build a monument to the brave heroes; the phallic, firehose-inspired concrete Coit Tower at the peak of Telegraph Hill was the result. You can ascend the 212ft column for impressive views across the city, provided there isn't too much fog. Otherwise, it's still worth trekking up the hill just to enjoy the well-preserved frescoes that decorate the interior of the tower's base, executed by students of the Mexican communist artist Diego Rivera. The intense, somber WPA murals were highly controversial and branded left wing when unveiled – they certainly reflect the preoccupations of the Depression era (work, work, and more work), though it's ironic that the few women seen are either shopping or picking flowers on a farm. Note Raymond Bertrand's *Meat Industry*, in which the artist cleverly adapts the building's windows to his sausage-smoking scene. The most direct path up the hill is on its western side along Filbert Street – a steepish

PLACES

Nob Hill, Russian Hill, and Telegraph Hill

EATING & DRINKING					
1550 Hyde Café & Wine Bar	13	Luella	6	Piperade	7
Boulange de Polk	5	Matterhorn	10	Sushi Groove	12
Fog City Diner	1	Nick's Crispy Tacos	8	Swan Oyster Depot	9
La Foile	5	Nook	11	Tablespoon	15
		Petit Robert		Tonga Room & Hurricane Bar	
		Pier 23			

Tonic	2	
Top of the Mark	16	
Yabbie's Coastal Kitchen	4	

ten-minute climb with good views on the way.

Filbert and Greenwich steps

The eastern face of Telegraph Hill is a rustic, idyllic enclave of low-slung old houses hidden behind leafy, overhanging gardens. No wonder the simple cottages here have skyrocketed in value in recent years – the views across the bay are astonishing. You can best enjoy them by descending on foot eastward down from the summit, through the crisscrossing, maze-like walkways that are etched into the side of the hill and connect the clusters of homes. The best-known routes are the Greenwich Steps, which cling to the hill at a 45-degree angle, and the more meandering

▼ COIT TOWER

Filbert Steps, which plateau at Montgomery Street in a leafy garden. Here you'll find a handful of simple houses that were built by 1850s Gold Rush immigrants and somehow survived the 1906 fire; dart off to one side along Napier Lane, famous as one of the last boardwalk streets in San Francisco and lined with bucolic cottages.

Levi Strauss Visitor Center

Levi's Plaza, 1155 Battery Street at Filbert ☎415/501-3295, ⓦwww .levistrauss.com. Daily 10am–5pm. Free. The ugly brick office complex here is the world HQ for Levi Strauss, the local jean genius who made a fortune making miners' pants in the Gold Rush. The lobby of the main building here hosts an exhibit–cum–visitor center dedicated to an aspect of Levi's culture or history: of course, it's mostly an extended shill (complete with map to the store in Union Square), but the vintage pants from the 1890s are a highlight.

San Francisco Art Institute

800 Chestnut St at Leavenworth ☎415/771-7020, ⓦwww .sanfranciscoart.edu. This low-rise Mission-style building, a working school whose alumni include Jerry Garcia, clings to the side of a steep street on Russian Hill. It's easy to miss, but make sure to seek out the institute's one notable artwork in the Diego Rivera Gallery – an outstanding, muscular mural by the artist. *The Making of a Fresco Showing the Building of a City* was executed in 1931 when he was at the height of his fame. Rivera's the chubby, dark-haired figure with his back to the viewer in the center of the painting.

Lombard Street

Russian Hill's Lombard Street is famed as San Francisco's twistiest street and looks like a terra-cotta-tiled water chute for cars. With eight tight curves between Hyde and Leavenworth, there's a 5mph speed limit – not that you'll be able to drive much faster given how many others are usually there to enjoy the drive – but you can also pick your way down on foot via the stepped sidewalk. The best time to enjoy it is early morning or, better still, late at night when the city lights twinkle below and the tourists have gone; photographs are more impressive taken from the foot, rather than the summit, of the hill.

▼ LOMBARD STREET

The French Village

Upper Polk Street on Russian Hill is the site on an inexplicable but endearing outpost where you can *vive la France*: there are three French restaurants, a lingerie shop, a French antiques outlet and even a French real estate agent, though were the local Realtor truly French, he wouldn't have dubbed his outfit Maison Nouveau, but rather Maison Nouvelle. Grammar goofs aside, it's a fun strip to browse – see below for listings.

Cable Car Museum

1201 Mason St at Washington ☏415/474-1997, ⊛www .cablecarmuseum.org. April–Sept daily 10am–6pm, Oct–March daily 10am–5pm; free. Essentially an indoor viewing platform for the innards of the system's engineering, rather than a resting home for retired carriages, this Nob Hill museum is a worthwhile stop thanks to the informative placards that will help even the least mechanically minded understand how cable cars work. The gift shop's also a fine place for fun souvenirs.

Grace Cathedral

1100 California St at Jones ☏415/749-6300, ⊛www .gracecathedral.org, Sun–Fri 7am–6pm, Sat 8am–6pm. Episcopal Grace Cathedral is one of the biggest hulks of neo-Gothic architecture in the US. A rather bland and disappointing copy of Notre Dame in Paris, it was begun after the 1906 fire but took until the early 1960s to finish – a fact sadly evident in its hodgepodge of poured concrete styles. The cathedral's notable for three things: first, for the fact that George W. Bush's ancestor Godwin was pastor here for awhile; second, for the copies of Ghiberti's Renaissance-inducing doors from the Florence Baptistry on its main entrance, included for no reason other than that they were available to the architect; and finally, for the cozy AIDS Interfaith Chapel with its vibrant cast-bronze altarpiece by the late pop art visionary Keith Haring.

Shops

ab fits

1519 Grant Ave at Union ☏415/982-5726, ⊛www.abfits.com. Closed Mon. Imaginative men's and women's boutique offering directional casual and jeanswear from the likes of Josh Podoll, J. Lindeberg, SBU, and Seven at moderate prices. Branch: 40 Grant Ave, Union Square ☏415/391-3360.

Cris

2056 Polk St at Broadway ☏415/474-1191. High-end consignment store, crammed with pristine designer garments from recent seasons at reasonable prices for men and women.

▼ CABLE CAR MUSEUM

Les Cent Culottes

1504 Vallejo St at Polk ☎415/614-2586, ⓦwww.lescentculottes.com. Closed Mon. The name of this all-French lingerie store means "100 Panties" – it's the place to come for upscale women's underwear, whether skimpy or supportive.

Old Vogue

1412 Grant Ave at Green ☎415/392-1522. Pricey vintage store with a wide men's selection and piles of good-as-new jeans on the upper mezzanine.

Smoke Signals

2223 Polk St at Green ☎415/292-6025 ⓔsmokesignls@aol.com. Terrific, encyclopedic newsstand stocking obscure magazines, Euro periodicals, and, of course, cigars and cigarettes.

Velvet Da Vinci

2015 Polk St at Pacific ☎415/441-0109. Sumptuous jewelry store–cum–gallery that stocks

art pieces by more than fifty designers from ten countries.

Cafés

La Boulange de Polk

2310 Polk St at Green ☎415/345-1107. Tues–Sat 7am–7pm, Sun to 6pm. Flaky croissants and crusty breads are the specialty at this new French bakery – there are a few seats if you want to sit and eat.

Nick's Crispy Tacos

1500 Broadway at Polk ☎415/409-8226. Campy cheapie café: the room's festooned with a piñata, mirror-ball, chandeliers, and sombreros for a too-much-is-never-enough Mexican fiesta. The crowd's refreshingly diverse, old and young, and the food's Anglo-friendly – burritos ($4.95–6.95) and tacos ($2.75–3.75).

Nook

1500 Hyde St at Jackson ☎415/447-4100. Homey corner café with sleek cream walls and dark wood tables. Try a snack like the herby ham, fontina, and sage baguette or a plate of grapevine tomatoes with mozzarella ($6–7); wine's $2.50 a glass during daily happy hour.

Restaurants

Fog City Diner

1300 Battery St at Filbert ☎415/982-2000, ⓦwww.fogcitydiner.com. Upscale, retro diner with Art Deco–ish fixtures that's a firm local landmark, offering quirky tweaks on traditional recipes like mascarpone brioche French toast and chicken hash with lobster (more succulent than it sounds).

▼ LE BOULANGE DE POLK

La Folie

2316 Polk St at Green ☏415/776-5577. Sumptuous Provençal food served without attitude or pretension. Choose a set meal: three- ($54), four- ($75) or five-course ($85), usually including frogs' legs, *assiette de boeuf* or Dungeness crab napoleon.

Luella

1896 Hyde St at Green ☏415/674-4343. Small family-run restaurant decked out in soothing mint green with crisp white tablecloths (nab the cozy booth for six by the bar). The modern American menu is inventive and tasty: mains run around $20 – don't miss the Coca-Cola-braised pork.

Matterhorn

2323 Van Ness Ave at Green ☏415/885-6116. Hidden in an apartment building, this authentically Swiss restaurant (the kitschy ski lodge–style decor was shipped here in pieces from the motherland) is known for its fondues, whether cheese, beef, or chocolate. The standout's undeniably the Fondue Ticinese, a thick and spicy blend of cheeses, pepperoncini, and tomatoes.

Petit Robert

2300 Polk St at Green ☏415/922-8100. Atmospheric French bistro offering mostly tapas-style *petits plats* for $5–14.50 – the steak tartare is superb.

Piperade

1015 Battery St at Green ☏415/391-2555, ⓦwww.piperade.com. Basque restaurant with rustic, wooden tables and a robust menu including cod in smoky broth and the namesake, ratatouille-esque stew; entrees cost $15–17. The warm atmosphere and the affable, attentive service are big pluses.

Sushi Groove

1916 Hyde St at Union ☏415/440-1905. Groovy, throbbing modern sushi restaurant offering quirky maki-roll combinations and unmissable sake martinis, all to a background of loud house music. Shame about the sloppy service.

Swan Oyster Depot

1517 Polk St at California ☏415/673-1101. No frills at this cheap seafood counter in Polk Gulch, but it's beloved by locals for the fiercely fresh fish. A meaty shrimp cocktail's just $7.

Tablespoon

2209 Polk St at Vallejo ☏415/268-0140. Pricey fusion restaurant, combining American, French, and Asian influences (pork tenderloin or offbeat Hawaiian fish at $17–20 per plate, for example). Make sure to try one of their housemade wine mojitos and to save room for desserts like rhubarb soup or roast grape and pistachio pizza.

Yabbie's Coastal Kitchen

2237 Polk St at Green ☏415/474-4088. Shellfish of every variety served in every way imaginable in an old-fashioned setting; oysters chilled on the half shell are the specialty (and only cost a buck each Sun–Wed 6–6.30pm). The prices are as high as the quality, with entrees from $15.95.

Bars

1550 Hyde Café and Wine Bar

1550 Hyde St at Jackson ☏415/775-1550, ⓦwww.1550hyde.com. The menu here is organic and

▲ THE TONGA ROOM

Mediterranean with a focus on local suppliers. The real draw, though, is its extensive wine list, with 26 regional wines by the glass.

Pier 23

Pier 23 ☎415/362-5125. Sit out on the deck under the heat lamps and enjoy cocktails by the bay, plus tasty Creole snacks. Thursday's a real scene, thanks to a raucous after-work crowd. Cover at weekends $8-10.

Tonga Room & Hurricane Bar

inside the *Fairmont Hotel*, 950 Mason St at California ☎415/772-5278 ⓦwww.fairmont.com. Basement Tiki lounge with grass huts and a floating band at night, not to mention an indoor rainstorm every fifteen minutes.

Tonic

2360 Polk St at Green ☎415/771-5535. A happening little pick-up joint, dark and chic, serving cheap mixed drinks (PBR or Miller is just $2 on Sundays) at a long mahogany bar. The trivia night on Wednesday is a blast.

Top of the Mark

inside the *Mark Hopkins Hotel*, 999 California St at Mason ☎415/392-3434, ⓦwww.markhopkins.net. The most famous of the city's rooftop bars, with sweeping views from the summit of Nob Hill, was founded in 1939 and still retains its old-world elegance. Try the trademark Top of the Mark cocktail – vodka and vermouth, served with a pickled green tomato. $5–10 cover for live music.

Fisherman's Wharf and Alcatraz

San Francisco's northern waterfront is dominated by the city's number-one-crowd-puller, Fisherman's Wharf. Each year, millions of visitors plow through its overpriced commercial gimmickry for a glimpse of what remains of a nearly obsolete fishing industry (these days the few fishermen that can afford the exorbitant mooring charges are usually done with their work before visitors arrive). There's ultimately little that's appealing about this tourist magnet (aside from a number of admittedly excellent restaurants) with one major exception – Alcatraz, the fabled island prison and one of San Francisco's unmissable sights.

Fisherman's Wharf

Piers 39, 41, 43, 43 1/2, and 45, ⓦwww.fishermanswharf.org. Despite its tacky reputation, the wharf is a massively popular tourist destination – creative interpretation of statistics allows it to claim to be the most visited attraction anywhere in America. If you join the millions flocking to the waterfront, it's best to avoid weekends and try to stop by as early as possible before the tour buses take over. Amid the souvenir stands, hot dog carts, and tourist tackiness, there's one amusing exception: the freaky Bush Man. In season, he can usually be found lurking, comically unhidden behind a bush on a pole, on the walkway near Pier 43, leaping out periodically to startle passersby, who drop a steady stream of change into his bucket. As for that honking noise, it's a colony of adolescent male sea lions that's taken over the floating platforms at sea level between Piers 39 and 41; the creatures are protected by the Marine Mammal Act and so are free to come and go as they please – just make sure not to feed them, as that's illegal.

Ghirardelli Square

900 North Point St at Larkin ⓣ415/775-5500, ⓦwww.ghirardellisq .com. Sun–Thurs 10am–6pm, Fri & Sat 10am–9pm Marking the western edge of Fisherman's Wharf, Ghirardelli Square is one of two old factories in the area that have been converted into boutiquey malls (The Cannery, 2801 Leavenworth St at Jefferson, ⓦwww .delmontesquare.com, is the other). Now housing a bland selection of stores alongside some surprisingly good restaurants, it was originally the headquarters of failed '49er and candy magnate Domenico Ghirardelli, who first discovered how to sweat the butter from raw cocoa and revolutionized the chocolate-making industry – making himself a millionaire thanks to the brown gold. The square itself is currently

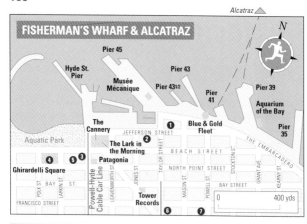

FISHERMAN'S WHARF & ALCATRAZ

Alcatraz

N

Pier 45
Hyde St. Pier
Musée Mécanique
Pier 43
Pier 43½
Pier 41
Pier 39
Aquarium of the Bay
Pier 35
THE EMBARCADERO

The Cannery
Blue & Gold Fleet ❶
JEFFERSON STREET
❷ The Lark in the Morning
Patagonia
Aquatic Park
BEACH STREET
TAYLOR STREET
❹ ❻❸
Ghirardelli Square
NORTH POINT STREET
Powell-Hyde Cable Car Line
JONES ST.
MASON ST.
POWELL ST.
BAY STREET
STOCKTON ST.
GRANT AVE.
KEARNY ST.
POLK ST.
LARKIN ST.
BAY ST.
FRANCISCO STREET
LEAVENWORTH ST.
Tower Records
❻
❼
0   400 yds

EATING & DRINKING

Ana Mandara	4	Buena Vista Café	3	Gary Danko	5
Boudin Sourdough		Café Francisco	7	In-n-Out Burger	2
Bakery & Café	1	Frjtz	4	The Mandarin	4
				McCormick & Kuleto's	4
				Pat's Café	6

undergoing changes that will see chunks of it morph into high-end condos and new stores pop up in some of the vacant units, but the full transformation's some time off.

Musée Mécanique

Pier 45 at Taylor St ☎415/386-1170. Mon–Fri 11am–7pm, Sat & Sun 10am–8pm. The Musée Mécanique is an oddball collection of historic arcade games, mixing retro arcade classics like Pac-Man with faux fortune tellers and the museum's best-known holding, Laughing Sal, a painted lady who looks like a horror-movie clown and will cackle fearsomely every time you deposit 25 cents. Entrance is free, but you'll need plenty of quarters to properly enjoy the games.

Aquarium of the Bay

Pier 39 at Beach and Stockton streets. ☎1-888/732-3483, ⓦwww.aquariumofthebay.com. Winter

▼ THE CANNERY

Mon–Fri 10am–6pm, Sat & Sun 10am–7pm; summer daily 9am–8pm. $13.95, $7 kids. Despite the stagy elevator ride that "dives" you to the bottom of the sea, the aquarium is still worth a visit thanks to the spectacular close-up views of fish and crustaceans that surround you as you trundle slowly along a 400ft acrylic viewing tunnel. The other must-see (or -do) is a petting pool where visitors can actually touch leopard sharks and bat rays.

Fort Mason

Fort Mason is a schizophrenic, sprawling park-cum-museum complex up a steep hill at the western end of the wharf. There are rolling green lawns here as well as old wharves now repurposed as theatres and museums. Originally a defense bulkhead during the earliest Spanish settlement, it became a US Army bastion during the Civil War and then a temporary home for the homeless in the wake of the 1906 earthquake and fire.

It was turned over to public use in the 1970s and is now divided into two areas: Upper Fort Mason on the hilltop is copse-dotted parkland, while Lower Fort Mason is home to old warehouses and wharves that have been turned into arts spaces: the best is the appealing Museo Italo-Americano in Building C (☎415/673-2200, ⓦwww.museoitaloamericano .org; Wed–Sun noon–4pm; $3, free and open noon–7pm first Wed of the month), home to a rotating collection of Italian arts and crafts.

Alcatraz

☎415/705-5555, ⓦwww.nps .gov/alcatraz. The black, crusty island visible from the wharf is Alcatraz, nicknamed "The Rock." For the first half of the twentieth century, this twelve-acre islet was America's most dreaded high-security prison and home to brand-name criminals like Al Capone and Machine Gun Kelly. The Prison on the Rock was notorious for its isolation: though it's only 1.25 miles from the city, the six-knot current in the Bay is so fierce that even strong swimmers had no hope of successful escape (nine men tried, none succeeded). The government shut down the jail in 1963 for financial reasons; when it reopened as a tourist attraction a few years later, Alcatraz went from money pit to potential gold mine – now, 750,000 visitors pass through each year. As for the Rock's curious name, it's Spanglish from alcatraces, or pelicans, birds that were common in the bay when the first European settlers arrived.

Once on the island, most people opt to use the hour-long self-guided audio tours, which provide sharp anecdotal commentary about life and events in the prison, mostly voiced by former inmates and guards. Skip the dull twelve-minute introductory film at the dock – if you want to learn more, join one of the lively, free ranger talks that run on a rolling schedule: the day's topics and times are marked on a whiteboard on the wall by the dock.

The island itself is surprisingly small up close, and the ramshackle cottages dotted around the main prison building make it look like an old Mediterranean fishing port – albeit one plastered with blaring federal signs. Once inside, though, it's easy to understand how emotionally grueling a stay on the Rock must have been – the bare cells are spartan and tiny, while the windowless isolation pens are pitch-black once the door is closed.

Blue and Gold Fleet boats (℡415/773-1188, ⓦwww .blueandgoldfleet.com; $16.50 including audio tour) depart from Pier 41, beginning at 9.30am, last boat back at 4.30pm. The best boats to catch are the first, when the jail's not yet packed with other tourists and will be evocatively empty, or the last, which offers a stunning view of the sunset in wintertime. Note that whatever boat you plan to catch, reservations are essential – book at least two weeks ahead in peak season, and about one week in advance during off season.

Shops

The Lark in the Morning
inside The Cannery, 2801 Leavenworth St at Beach ℡415/922-4277, ⓦwww .larkinam.com. Mind-bendingly eclectic musical instrument store, stocking global oddities from Africa, Asia, and Australia like the Ethiopian thighbone trumpet; even better, you can try before you buy.

▼ ALCATRAZ

Patagonia
770 North Point at Hyde ℡415/771-2050. This store, with its functional performance clothing, could lay claim to being the patron saint of Bay Area outdoor enthusiasts. Prices are fair, and many products have more of a fashion sensibility than you'll find at other sportswear stores.

Tower Records
2525 Jones St at Columbus Ave ℡415/885-0500. Local megastore, with a huge classical annex across the street.

Cafés

Boudin Sourdough Bakery & Café
160 Jefferson St at Mason ℡415/928-1849, ⓦwww.boudinbakery.com. The sandwiches here feature this chain's signature local sourdough bread, made using a 150-year-old recipe; the café's now attached to a working bakery that the company's opened as a see-and-taste museum, though it's only for devotees.

Café Francisco
2161 Powell St at Francisco ℡415/397-2602. Cheap neighborhood café that's great for a lazy breakfast on a sunny day, especially when taken at one of the outdoor tables.

Frjtz
inside Ghirardelli Square, 900 North Point at Larkin ℡415/928-3886, ⓦwww .frjtzfries.com. Groovy mosaic-strewn *friterie*, with indoor and outdoor tables serving cones of crunchy Belgian-style fries with dips like tabasco-chive ketchup or spicy yogurt

peanut (small $3 with one dip, large $4.50 with two dips), as well as savory crepes named after artists – try the El Greco with feta, spinach and tomatoes.

In-n-Out Burger

333 Jefferson St at Jones ⓦwww .in-n-out.com. Local outpost of the West Coast ethical burger joint (higher than minimum wages and good working conditions) that's a foodie cult fave outside California for those who can't stop by every weekend for a quick fix. Make a pilgrimage here to try its meaty hamburger "animal style," with lettuce, pickle, tomato, and grilled onions, as well as the sloppy, old-fashioned milkshakes.

Pat's Café

2320 Taylor at Columbus ☎415/776-8735, ⓦwww.patscafe.com. Bright, artwork-crammed café with simple Formica tables and a short menu of burgers and sandwiches from $4.50. The garlic, lime, and cilantro fries are delicious.

Restaurants

Gary Danko

800 North Point St at Hyde ☎415/749-2060, ⓦwww.garydanko .com. The poshest restaurant in San Francisco, serving an adventurous, ever-changing American menu – it's definitely performance food, as each dish is unveiled from beneath a silver *cloche* with a determined flourish. At $79 (plus $45 for wine pairing), the four-course tasting menu is an unforgettable, if wallet-busting, experience.

The Mandarin

in Ghirardelli Square, 900 North Point ☎415/673-8812, ⓦwww.themandarin .com. Authentic, upscale Chinese food in a lush, hushed dining room – try the kung pao chicken ($14.95) or the surprisingly tender, tasty sweet-and-sour pork ($15.95).

McCormick and Kuleto's

in Ghirardelli Square, 900 North Point St at Larkin ☎415/929-1730, ⓦwww.mccormickandschmicks.com. Old-school fish restaurant that serves reliable, sometimes even exceptional, seafood: the salmon gravlax is delicious, as are the coconut prawns wth papaya mango salsa. Expect to pay around $20 per entrée.

Bars

Ana Mandara

in Ghirardelli Square, 891 Beach St at Polk ☎415/771-6800, ⓦwww .anamandara.com. The beautiful, bamboo-decorated Cham Bar and Lounge at this upscale restaurant is a soothing place to listen to live jazz and sip a cocktail.

Buena Vista Café

2765 Hyde St at Beach ☎415/474-5044, ⓦwww.thebuenavista.com. The place that invented Irish coffee (or so they say) – try a whiskey-soaked, cream-topped cup or two at this divey pub and see how the original ranks against every other foamy boozy version you've tried.

Pacific Heights and the northern waterfront

Perched on steep hills, the millionaires' neighborhood of Pacific Heights is home to some of the city's most monumental Victorian piles and stone mansions. The area's architectural uniformity is due to its late development, since the hilly terrain could only be colonized once gradient-conquering cable-car lines had linked it to downtown. Close by, in the northern districts of the Marina and Cow Hollow, are the manicured haunts and well-appointed apartments of San Francisco's upwardly mobile young professionals, as well as, not surprisingly, a good selection of upscale bars and restaurants. Immediately south of the Heights stands Japantown, an artificially created enclave that houses much of the city's sizable Japanese community. It's a terrific place, not only for cheap sushi but to browse for Asian art or pick up a Japanese pop CD or two.

▼ HAAS-LILIENTHAL HOUSE

Haas-Lilienthal House

2007 Franklin St at Washington
☎ 415/441-3004, ⊛ www.sfheritage
.org. 1hr tours leave every 20–30min,
Wed & Sat noon–3pm, Sun 11am–
4pm. $8. An ornate, double-size
Queen Anne–style home
that was built for his growing
family by a wealthy merchant,
William Haas, this house is a
grand symbol of old wealth,
with intricate wooden towers
outside and Tiffany art glass
and stenciled leather paneling
inside. It's worth stopping by to
poke around the well-preserved
interior, though the talky tours
are more illuminating about
the family's day-to-day life
than about the architecture of
the building, an eye-catching
example of the city's Victorian
style.

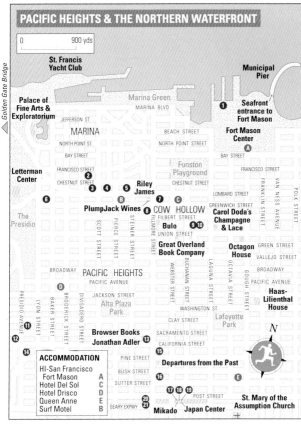

PACIFIC HEIGHTS & THE NORTHERN WATERFRONT

0   900 yds

Golden Gate Bridge

St. Francis Yacht Club

Municipal Pier

Palace of Fine Arts & Exploratorium

Marina Green

Seafront entrance to Fort Mason

MARINA BLVD

JEFFERSON ST.

MARINA

BEACH STREET

Fort Mason Center

NORTH POINT ST.

NORTH POINT STREET

Letterman Center

BAY STREET

BAY STREET

FRANCISCO STREET

Funston Playground

FRANCISCO STREET

CHESTNUT STREET

CHESTNUT STREET

Riley James

The Presidio

PlumpJack Wines

COW HOLLOW

FILBERT STREET

LOMBARD STREET

GREENWICH STREET

Carol Doda's Champagne & Lace

VAN NESS AVENUE

FRANKLIN STREET

POLK STREET

Bulo

UNION STREET

SCOTT STREET

PIERCE STREET

STEINER STREET

FILLMORE STREET

Great Overland Book Company

Octagon House

GREEN STREET

VALLEJO STREET

BROADWAY

PACIFIC HEIGHTS

PACIFIC AVENUE

JACKSON STREET

WEBSTER STREET

BUCHANAN STREET

LAGUNA STREET

OCTAVIA STREET

GOUGH STREET

BROADWAY

PACIFIC AVENUE

Haas-Lilienthal House

PRESIDIO AVENUE

LYON STREET

BAKER STREET

BRODERICK STREET

DIVISADERO STREET

Alta Plaza Park

WASHINGTON ST.

CLAY STREET

Lafayette Park

N

Browser Books

Jonathan Adler

SACRAMENTO STREET

CALIFORNIA STREET

ACCOMMODATION

PINE STREET

Departures from the Past

HI-San Francisco Fort Mason	A
Hotel Del Sol	C
Hotel Drisco	D
Queen Anne	E
Surf Motel	B

BUSH STREET

SUTTER STREET

POST STREET

St. Mary of the Assumption Church

GEARY EXPWY

Mikado   Japan Center

EATING & DRINKING

415 Baker Street Bistro	6	Boom Boom Room	20	Mamacita	3
A16	2	City Tavern	7	On the Bridge	19
Ace Wasabi's Rock 'n' Roll Sushi	5	Ella's	14	Patisserie Delanghe	16
		The Fillmore	21	Perry's	10
Asian Restaurant & Lounge	12	G Bar	11	Perry's Joint	20
Betelnut	9	Greens	1	Pizza Orgasmica	8
Bistro Yoffi	4	The Grove	15	Sapporo-ya	17
Bittersweet	13	Maki	18		

St Mary of the Assumption

1111 Gough St at Geary ☏415/567-2020, ⊛www.stmarycathdralsf.org. Mon–Fri 6.45am–4.30pm, Sat 6.45am–6.30pm, Sun 7.30am–4.45pm. Built in 1971 to replace a fire-damaged predecessor, this stunning piece of modernist architecture in lower Pacific Heights has unfairly been derided by local wags for supposedly resembling a washing-machine agitator (thus its nickname, "Our Lady of the Maytag"). Make sure to stop inside to see its swooping, vaulted interior that seems to swirl with movement and the

▲ ST MARY OF THE ASSUMPTION

in internment camps during World War II – is now the center of a densely concentrated Japanese community of around 12,000 people who keep the food, record, and book stores here in brisk business. The major sight is the 100-foot Peace Pagoda, which stands in the outdoor central plaza that links the main buildings and looks like a stack of poured-concrete space-age mushrooms. Another peaceful refuge in the Center is the Kabuki Hot Springs, 1750 Geary Blvd at Fillmore (☎1-866/218-8077, ⓦwww.kabukisprings.com, $16–20 entry fee), a soothing traditional Japanese bathhouse that's been funked up by its new owners but still retains some of the spa's original eccentricity.

impressive organ that looks like a pin cushion with a mohawk.

Japan Center

Post St between Fillmore and Laguna streets ☎415/922-6776.
A sprawling shopping mall that was built in 1968 as a conciliatory gesture toward the local Japanese community – many of whom had, like other Japanese-Americans, been held

Chestnut Street

The area known as the Marina, the mother lode for San Francisco's yuppie techie types, centers on Chestnut Street, a strip of shops, restaurants, and lounges that has a (deserved) reputation as a haven for swinging singles. The local watering holes are known as

Victorians

Built in the second half of the nineteenth century from once-plentiful redwoods culled from the Marin headlands to the north, these fancy mansions fell out of popularity with the arrival of Art Deco in the 1920s, and many were demolished as part of the vogue for urban redevelopment in the 1960s. Those that survived – and there are around 13,500 **Victorians** in San Francisco proper – are now highly sought after by nostalgic (and wealthy) young home buyers. There are three main styles: Italianate, marked out by the use of Corinthian columns; Stick, signaled by the decorative vertical "sticks" appliquéd to the facade; and Queen Anne, with roof gables and turrets. Note that the lurid color schemes with which they're so associated are an anachronism: originally painted entirely pale green or white, some Victorians took on their Technicolor hues when hippies, who'd moved into abandoned or unloved mansions in nearby Haight-Ashbury, were allowed to paint their homes psychedelic colors by grateful, money-saving landlords. Very quickly, houses across the city – even in conservative Pacific Heights – followed suit.

"high-intensity breeder bars," and the neighborhood's massive Safeway has a pick-up scene so fierce it's been dubbed, without a trace of irony, "The Body Shop." The Marina's one of the least earthquake-proof parts of the city, since it's built entirely on landfill in an area that was artificially reclaimed from the sea in 1915 to house the Panama Pacific International Exhibition.

Union Street

This is the main artery through the district of Cow Hollow, which was once a small valley of pastures and dairies in the post–Gold Rush years (hence the name). The stretch between Van Ness and Divisadero holds one of the city's densest concentrations of boutiques and cafés; it buzzes with neighborhood shoppers, especially on weekends, and it's a pleasant place to amble for an afternoon.

Octagon House Museum

2645 Gough St at Union ☎415/441-7512. Second Sun, second and fourth Thurs of each month, noon–3pm; closed January. Donation suggested. The work of Orson Fowler, a nineteenth-century eccentric who published a book extolling the virtues of eight-sided living, was the inspiration for this oddball building in Cow Hollow. It's hard to miss, sitting defiantly in the middle of a small park, a neat blue-and-white relic of a long-forgotten fad (Fowler claimed eight-sided living was the answer to good health and long life). This particular octagonal home was built in 1861 by a local farmer, William McElroy, who stashed a time capsule under the stairs that was discovered during

recent renovations; now on display, it offers a captivating glimpse at everyday life in early San Francisco, including letters, photographs, and a contemporary newspaper.

Palace of Fine Arts

Marina Boulevard and Baker Street ☎415/563-6504, ⊛www .palaceoffinearts.org. Despite its name, this isn't a museum, but rather a huge, freely interpreted classical ruin that was first erected for the Panama Pacific International Exhibition held in the Marina in 1915. When all the other buildings from the temporary Exhibition were torn down, the palace was saved simply because locals thought it too beautiful to destroy. Unfortunately, since it was built of wood, plaster, and burlap, the palace gradually crumbled until the late 1950s, when a wealthy resident put up money for the structure to be recast in reinforced concrete. To the modern eye, it's a moody and mournfully sentimental piece of Victoriana, complete with weeping figures on the colonnade representing the melancholy of life without art. (The originals are now in the Exploratorium nearby.)

Exploratorium

3601 Lyon St at Baker. Information ☎415/563-7337, Tactile Dome reservations ☎415/561-0362, ⊛www.exploratorium.edu. Tues–Sun 10am–5pm, $13 ($3 additional charge for Tactile Dome), free first Wed of the month. Hands-down the best kid-centric attraction in the city, this museum crams more than 650 hands-on exhibits into a small warehouse space, each of which helps explain the principles of electricity or sound waves or similar. It's renowned for the Tactile Dome, a total sensory deprivation chamber, explored on hands and knees – and not for the claustrophobic (reservations essential). Note that at time of writing, the museum was eyeing a move to digs twice its current size on Pier 15 at the Embarcadero; the move's almost certain to be confirmed, but a time line has yet to be released.

The Presidio

It's little wonder that this vast wilderness park, which stretches across almost 1500 acres, is so craggy and unspoiled – it started out as a military base. Now open to all (and even home to Yoda and Co. – see box below), the Presidio is a more rural alternative for a bike ride or hike than the manicured lawns of Golden Gate Park; stroll or cycle along part of the Pacific Coast Trail here for the not-to-be-missed views across the bay and back to the skyline. The park's main entrance for drivers, cyclists, and pedestrians is from Lombard and Lyon streets; the huge gate there leads to the main quadrangle of buildings that once functioned as a military headquarters and are currently under renovation through mid-2007 at least. While its permanent quarters in Building 102 are spruced up, the Presidio Museum's in a temporary spot, the Officers Club, or Building 50, on Moraga Avenue (Ⓦwww.nps.gov/prsf). It showcases so-so military memorabilia alongside fascinating maps showing which parts of the city were worst affected by the 1906 earthquake and fire.

Golden Gate Bridge

☎415/921-5858, Ⓦwww.goldengate.org. As much an architectural as an engineering feat, the Golden Gate Bridge took just over four years to build and opened to traffic in 1937. It was the world's first massive suspension bridge, with a span of 4200 feet, and was designed to withstand winds of up to 100 miles an hour and to swing as much as 27 feet. Its ruddy color (known as International Orange) was originally intended as a temporary undercoat before the gray topcoat was applied, but locals liked it so much the bridge has stayed orange ever since – and it takes more than 5000 gallons of paint annually to keep it that way. You can either drive, bike, or walk across: the toll for southbound cars is $5, although biking is more thrilling as you teeter along under the bridge's towers. It takes about half an hour to walk the bridge's span, but it's an awe-inspiring amble,

---

Light sabers and rolling lawns

One man has finally managed to navigate the red tape and local opposition to any development in the Presidio: Star Wars guru **George Lucas**. In 2005, he moved his massive CGI operation from Skywalker Ranch in Marin to a $300m campus here known as the Letterman Center. The new buildings – none of which are open to the public – are scarcely distinguishable from their vintage counterparts, and there's no signage; the only evidence of Lucas is the small statue of Yoda out front. Look for the buildings immediately north of Lombard Street just inside the entrance.

▲ THE PACIFIC COAST TRAIL

what with the unbeatable views of the city and the craggy landscape of the Marin Headlands.

Shops

Browser Books

2195 Fillmore St at California ☎415/567-8027. This closetlike shop's full of the aroma of coffee from the café next door, mixed with old books – there are remainders and full-priced selections as well as a strong local section.

Bulo

3040 Fillmore St at Filbert ☎415/614-9959. This store sells quirky European shoes, with an earthy, retro feel. They're more functional than high fashion – think funky flats that'll easily handle the hills.

Carol Doda's Champagne & Lace

1850 Union St, no. 1, at Laguna ☎415/279-3666. Small boudoir-like store stocking Frederick's of Hollywood–style lacy lingerie personally selected by the Queen of Topless Waitressing, Carol Doda (see p.85).

The Great Overland Book Company

2848 Webster St at Union ☎415/351-1538. Cluttered with piles of books, this is a top-notch, old-fashioned store, featuring mint-condition first editions as well as cheap paperbacks.

Jonathan Adler

2133 Fillmore St at California ☎415/563-9500, ⓦwww .jonathanadler.com. New York–based potter Adler is known for his chic, understated homewares – expanding from simple vases in muted tones like beige and cream to soft goods and rugs in geometric patterns.

Mikado Japan Center

1737 Post St ☎415/922-9450. Enormous Japanese record emporium where the staff will let you watch DVDs or listen to a catchy CD by the latest Japanese pop star before you decide to buy.

PlumpJack Wines

3201 Fillmore St at Greenwich ☎415/346-9870, ⓦwww.plumpjack .com. The place to go if you're looking for an obscure Californian vintage or just a reliable local staple; the store has an enormous, exhaustive selection of in-state wines.

Riley James

3027 Fillmore St at Greenwich ☎415/775-7956. Trendy men's and women's bilevel designer store stocking the likes of Hollywould, Frost French, Chip & Pepper, and Fake London.

Cafés and snacks

Bittersweet

2123 Fillmore Street at California, ☎415/346-8715, ⓦwww .bittersweetcafe.com. Store-cum-café that's chocoholic heaven: buy a slab to go, or settle in at the bar for the choc-heavy cakes and drinks.

The Grove

2016 Fillmore St at California ☎415/474-1419. Eclectic and all-American upscale diner food including pressed sandwiches like a classic Reuben as well as comfort staples including lasagna and mac-'n'-cheese (all $7–9). The decor's inexplicably and vaguely southwestern, with ample comfy leather sofas.

Patisserie Delanghe

1890 Fillmore St at Bush ☎415/923-0711. Artisanal French bakery, run by two expats, who make flaky, buttery croissants and glistening fruit tarts for $2 or so – try the fruit brioche. There are a few tables in the window if you want to sit and eat.

Perry's Joint

1661 Fillmore St at Geary ☎415/931-5260. Unhurried, offbeat Japantown café, serving delicious Coney Island hot dogs ($3.50)

as well as dozens of flavors of ice cream.

Pizza Orgasmica

3157 Fillmore St at Greenwich ☎415/931-5300, ⓦwww .pizzaorgasmica.com. Cheapie pizza joint that's a delicious lunchtime pit stop, serving gourmet pies available by the slice. There are a few tables if you want to linger; settle in for awhile if you want to enjoy the $7.50 all-you-can-eat daily special (11am–4pm).

Sapporo-ya

1581 Webster St at Post ☎415/563-7400. Bustling and basic restaurant that offers delicious, low-cost buckwheat ramen – made on-site by the old-fashioned noodle machine on display in the window – served up in thick, flavorful miso or pork broths for less than $10.

Restaurants

(415) Asian Restaurant and Lounge

415 Presidio Ave at California ☎415/409-0400, ⓦwww .restaurant415.com. Improbably located in the Jewish Community Center, this newbie Japanese eatery serves sushi ($3.50–8.50), sashimi (five pieces of tuna for $10), and a few other creative options (BBQ chili short ribs for $21) to a Marina singles crowd. Grab a table on the balcony in the back – it's more private – and order a MoMo cocktail, with rum, black grapes, lime, and crunchy sugar.

Ace Wasabi's Rock 'n' Roll Sushi

3339 Steiner St at Lombard ☎415/567-4903, ⓦwww .acewasabissushi.com. Fast, cheap, and loud, dishing up a touch of rock-'n'-roll attitude with every order; stop by at 6pm weeknights to play bingo – the winner gets $20 off their bill. Ask for the delicious, off-menu dragon egg roll (spicy tuna, wrapped in avocado).

Baker Street Bistro

2953 Baker St at Lombard ☎415/931-1475, ⓦwww .bakerstbistro.citysearch.com. Cramped but charming French café with a few outdoor tables where the $14.50 prix fixe dinner is a bargain – it's usually soup and dessert plus a simple lamb chop or pork belly. It's hard to find, nestled on a Cow Hollow side street in the shadow of the Presidio.

Betelnut

2026 Union St at Buchanan ☎415/929-8855. Sceney local hangout, known for its offbeat Asian menu that's a hybrid of the dim sum and tapas traditions: you'll pay around $10 a plate for the likes of lychee tea–smoked quail.

Bistro Yoffi

2231 Chestnut St at Pierce ☎415/885-5133. Charming mid-price (mains $14–18) Marina bistro, packed with potted ferns and mismatched chairs, and serving eclectic modern American dishes. The chef's especially known for her skill with desserts – try the vanilla bean crème brûlée.

Ella's

500 Presidio Ave at California ☎415/441-5669, ⓦwww .ellassanfrancisco.com. The most notorious breakfast wait in town (90 minutes is the norm), so put on some comfortable shoes. It's worth hanging around, though, for the food, mostly Californian

interpretations of American classics like Mandarin pancakes with mango syrup for around $9.

Greens

Fort Mason Center, Building A ☎415/771-6222, ⓦwww .greensrestaurant.com. This is the queen of San Francisco's vegetarian restaurants. Upsides include its picturesque setting on a pier and adventurous dishes, like filo pastry layered with artichokes; downsides are the surly service and the unusually high prices for vegetarian dishes ($16–19 per entrée). Closed Monday lunch.

Maki

1825 Post St at Webster ☎415/921-5125. Japan Center restaurant specializing in *wappan meshi* – a wood steamer filled with vegetables, meat, and rice – but popular as much for its warm, friendly owner as for the food. Closed Monday.

Mamacita

2317 Chestnut St at Scott ☎415/346-8494, ⓦwww .mamacitasf.com. The crowd at this Mexican joint is young, eclectic, and rowdy, chugging down tangy, lime-heavy margaritas as well as flavorful modern takes on traditional dishes like *pollo asada* or crispy mahimahi tacos ($10 for three). Save room for the molten, mouth-tingling chocolate boudin ($7).

On the Bridge

1581 Webster St at Post ☎415/922-7765. Smallish Japan Center cafeteria serving *yoshoko*, or westernized Japanese food, such as spaghetti with *kimchee* (pickled cabbage) for around $8 a dish.

Bars

A16

2355 Chestnut St at Divisadero
☎415/771-2216, ⓦwww.a16sf.
com. Southern Italian restaurant
does double duty as a roomy
bar, with large windows over
the street and more than forty
different options of wine by the
glass. Try the flight of wines for
around $20.

City Tavern

3200 Fillmore St at Greenwich
☎415/567-0918. The best of
the yuppie haunts that dot
the Marina, this bar attracts
a youngish crowd of preppy,
clean-cut professionals. It's
the favored place to sip a
Chardonnay in a chic meat-
market setting.

Perry's

1944 Union St at Buchanan
☎415/922-9022. Made legendary
by Armistead Maupin's *Tales
of the City*, this low-lit Cow
Hollow institution is a hugely
popular sports pub and a
friendly place to grab a pint.

Clubs and live music

Boom Boom Room

1601 Fillmore St at Geary ☎415/673-
8000, ⓦwww.boomboomblues
.com. Gritty venue near Japan
Center that was owned by the
late bluesman John Lee Hooker
until his death in 2001 and
plays host to a fine selection of
touring blues and funk artists.
Cover $5–15.

The Fillmore Auditorium

1805 Geary St at Fillmore ☎415/346-
6000, ⓦwww.thefillmore.com. The
Fillmore was at the heart of
the 1960s counterculture and
reopened in 1994 after several
years' hiatus; it's home now to
rock and alt-rock touring acts.
Cover varies.

SoMa

SoMa (the area SOuth of MArket) had been an industrial wasteland from the city's earliest days but took an unimaginable upswing in the mid-1990s, thanks to Internet start-up companies that flocked to the district and its rock-bottom rents. SoMa's revival crashed alongside the dot-com dream in early 2000, forcing many restaurants and bars to close, but the area's slowly regaining its spark, especially due to a slew of hot nightclubs/restaurants along Brannan and Folsom streets as well as the new furniture showrooms that fill its western reaches. Note that despite the recent boom, there are still parts of SoMa that are downright dangerous even during the day (it's still scruffy enough to have doubled for early-1990s NYC in the recent movie version of Rent), so stay accordingly alert and keep valuables hidden, especially along Sixth Street.

GLBT Historical Society

657 Mission St, #300, at 3rd
ⓣ415/777-5455, ⓦwww.glbthistory
.org, Tues–Sat 1–5pm, free. Easily overlooked on the third floor of an office building, this is the only museum in town expressly dedicated to gay and lesbian history. There's a rotating space with new exhibitions every six months or so on aspects of gay life (sports was a recent topic) as well as an impressive archive open to all, including locker-room doors from 1970s-era bathhouses, the suit Harvey Milk was wearing when he was shot, Sylvester's Lycra-heavy stage outfits, and thousands of periodicals and 'zines. Make sure to call in advance if you have a particular interest.

▼ THE SWANK LOBBY AT THE *PALACE HOTEL*

SoMa PLACES

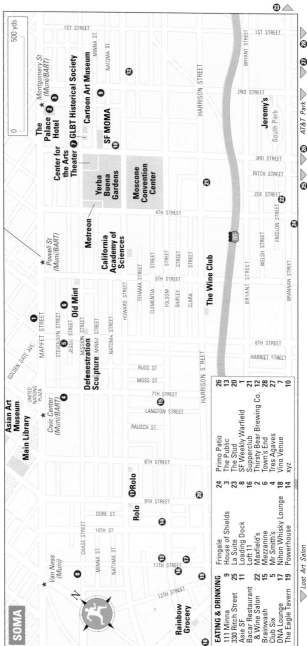

SOMA

500 yds

1ST STREET
MINNA ST.
NATOMA ST.

The Palace ★ Montgomery St
Hotel ② (Muni/BART)
③ GLBT Historical Society
Center for ⑦
the Arts Cartoon Art Museum
Theater ⑨
SF MOMA
Yerba ⑩
Buena
Gardens ⑫
Moscone
Convention ⑪
Center HARRISON STREET
Powell St
(Muni/BART) ★
Metreon 3RD STREET
RITCH STREET
ZOE STREET
California
Academy of
Sciences
4TH STREET
STREET
STREET
STREET
The Wine Club BRYANT STREET
WELSH STREET
FREELON STREET
BRANNAN STREET

1ST STREET
BRYANT STREET

Jeremy's
South Park

2ND STREET

AT&T Park

Asian Art
Museum
Main Library Mapfet STREET ①
GOLDEN GATE AVE.
UNITED STEVENSON STREET
NATIONS JESSE STREET Old Mint ⑥
PLAZA ④ ⑤ MISSION STREET
Civic Center Defenestration MINNA STREET
(Muni/BART) ★ Sculpture NATOMA STREET
HOWARD STREET
TEHAMA STREET
CLEMENTIA
5TH STREET FOLSOM
SHIPLEY
CLARA
RUSS ST.
MOSS ST.
7TH STREET 6TH STREET
⑮ HARRIET STREET
LANGTON STREET
RAUSCH ST. HARRISON STREET

8TH STREET

⑪ Rolo
Rolo
DORE ST.
9TH STREET ⑳
CHASE STREET
10TH ST. ⑭
MINNA ST.
NATOMA ST. ⑬
Van Ness ⑰
(Muni) 11TH STREET ⑲
N 12TH STREET

Rainbow
Grocery ⑯

② ③ ⑨ ⑫ ⑩ (map reference numbers)

EATING & DRINKING

111 Minna	9	Fringale	9
330 Ritch Street	25	House of Shields	13
Asia SF	11	La Suite	20
Bacar Restaurant		Loading Dock	1
& Wine Salon	22	Loft 11	16
Brainwash	15	Maxfield's	2
Club Six	5	Mezzanine	12
DNA Lounge	17	Mr Smith's	28
The Eagle Tavern	19	Powerhouse	7
		Primo Patio	24
		The Public	3
		The Stud	23
		SF Weekly Warfield	8
		Supperclub	21
		Thirsty Bear Brewing Co.	12
		Town's End	6
		Tres Agaves	4
		Nihon Whisky Lounge	18
		Vino Venue	27
		xyz	14
		Powerhouse	10

Lost Art Salon

Palace Hotel

Originally built in 1875, this palatial hotel (hence the name) at Market and Montgomery (see p.191) was a symbol of San Francisco's swaggering new wealth. It burned down during the 1906 fire but was lavishly reconstructed – and though subsequent renovations have dampened most of its glories, the Garden Court dining room, where you can enjoy high tea today, still boasts its original 1875 Austrian crystal chandeliers suspended from a ceiling made from 72,000 panes of glass.

Cartoon Art Museum

655 Mission St at New Montgomery ☎415/227-8669, ⓦ www.cartoonart .org; Tues–Sun 11am–5pm; $6. Housed in a massive slab concrete gallery space, this inventive museum curates rotating exhibits of cells and drawings, usually a sprightly mix of high-concept "art-oons" by the likes of French illustrator Moebius as well as staples like Peanuts.

Yerba Buena Gardens

Mission and 3rd streets ⓦ www .yerbabuenagardens.com; daily sunrise–10pm. Free. An iconic example of urban reclamation, these gardens are a rare instance of successful greenspace development. Not only has the circular park been seamlessly integrated into the surrounding area, but the inviting lawns and benches are often packed with picnicking office workers on warm weekday lunchtimes. Stretching along the park's eastern face is a magnificent fifty-foot granite waterfall memorial to Martin Luther King, Jr, inscribed with extracts from his speeches; on the terrace above lies a Sister Cities garden, featuring flora from each of the thirteen cities worldwide that is twinned with San Francisco.

San Francisco Museum of Modern Art

151 3rd St at Mission ☎415/357-4000, ⓦ www.sfmoma.org; Fri–Tues 11am–5.45pm, Thurs 11am–8.45pm, closed Wed. $12.50, $6.25 Thurs 6–8:45pm, free the first Tues of the month. SFMOMA is as famous for its premises as its collection; the striped building, with its sliced-off center turret looking like a black-and-white-striped

▼ THE MARTIN LUTHER KING JR. MEMORIAL WATERFALL

boiled egg, was designed by Swiss architect Mario Botta and built in 1995 at a reported cost of $62 million. Inside, the turret's skylight floods the space with light while you walk across vertigo-inducing slatted metal catwalks that connect the upper floors. Although Botta's bizarre landmark is undeniably showstopping, the museum's holdings are disappointing in comparison: highlights are its photographic print collection (look for Man Ray and Cartier-Bresson, among others) plus a strong showing of cult California School favorites like Diebenkorn, Frida Kahlo, and Diego Rivera and some snappy Pop Art pieces (Jeff Koons's gilded porcelain statue of Michael Jackson and Bubbles, for example). It's better to spend more time checking out the traveling exhibitions, which often supply the arty spark that's missing from the museum's own earnest holdings.

▼ THE SFMOMA

California Academy of Sciences

875 Howard St at 5th ☎415/321-8000, ⓦwww.calacademy.org. Daily 10am–5pm. $7, $5 third Thurs of every month 5–9pm. Having decamped from Golden Gate Park until late 2008 while its original site is radically rebuilt (see p.152), the academy's showcasing a smaller collection in a rugged, industrial setting that's unlikely to captivate adults but is a delight for kids. Rotating science exhibits spread across two floors and include the Nature's Nest, a themed playroom for the under-5 set. The Steinhart Aquarium also has a tiny home here until 2008. Among the clearly labeled modular tanks, each holding a different species, look for the garishly furry pink and white anemones and the shy piranhas lurking at the bottom of their tank.

Folsom Street

Though windswept and nondescript by day, this street fizzes with bars and clubs at night, especially those catering to the city's leather fetishists: if chaps and public whippings are your bag, make sure to book a trip back in late September for the Folsom Street Fair (between 8th and 11th streets ☎415/861-3247, ⓦwww.folsomstreetfair.com), a celebration of all things fetish.

Defenestration sculpture

214 6th St at Mission. A quixotic piece of public art by local artist Brian Goggin, involving furniture that has been bolted to the outside of an abandoned building – worth a detour for a quick photo during daylight hours, but don't linger too long as this is one of the nastier

corners in town. The current owners are rumored to be trying to sell the building for redevelopment, so catch this while you can.

AT&T Park

24 Willie Mays Plaza at 3rd and King streets ☏415/972-1800, ⓦsanfrancisco.giants.mlb.com. The state-of-the-art $357 million home for the San Francisco Giants is clearly an improvement over the team's old, bleak home at Candlestick Park. AT&T (originally Pac Bell, then, briefly, SBC) Park took only 28 months to build and made its debut on the opening day of the 2000 season. The stadium, in one of the sunniest parts of town, has the second shortest right field in major-league baseball (at 309 feet, only Fenway Park bests it). The outfield opens onto the bay, where, during games, kayakers lurk, waiting to catch home runs. In fact, permission was required from the League to allow the design, and many grumble that it was specifically intended to allow star Barry Bonds to hit home runs more easily. The anchor of the team and an All-Star outfielder, Bonds shot to fame by shattering the season home-run record (he hit 73 out of the park) and leading the Giants to their first World Series win since the 1980s in 2002. However, four years later, his reputation was lethally damaged by well-documented though unprovable allegations of chronic steroid abuse, and he'll now leave a tarnished legacy.

The season runs April–September, and tickets are a hot commodity; call a few weeks ahead to book one of the non-season seats; otherwise you can try to get one of the 500 bleacher seats that go on sale four hours in advance every game day (check the website for schedules, prices, and availability). If you can't snag a seat or are visiting in the wintertime, you can still see the inside of the stadium, walk on the field, and sit in the comfy padded dugout seats, thanks to the superb tours that leave from the dugout store on Third Street (☏415/972-2400, daily except on home-game days, 10.30am & 12.30pm, $10).

Shops

Jeremy's

2 South Park at 2nd ☏415/882-4929. Outstanding, bargain-packed consignment and secondhand store specializing in casual and designer clothes for men and women, seconds, and fashion-show outtakes.

▼ STATUE OF WILLIE MAYS AT AT&T PARK

Lost Art Saloon

245 South Van Ness at 13th, Suite 303 ☎415.861.1530 ⓦwww.lostartca.com. Tues & Thurs 12–8pm; other times by appointment. This kitschy gallery sells cheap, no-name pictures from the 1940s–1970s for $600 or less – the focus is on decorative arts rather than the cult surrounding painter.

Rainbow Grocery

1745 Folsom St at 13th ☎415/863-0620, ⓦwww.rainbowgrocery.coop. Progressive politics and organic food in this huge whole-food store.

Rolo

1235 Howard St at 8th ☎415/355-1122, ⓦwww.rolo.com; 1301 Howard St at 9th ☎415/861-1999. Funky, unisex retailer with one of the best, most browsable selections of casualwear in town: 1235 Howard stocks denim and streetwear (Rogan, WESC, Umbro by Kim Jones) while 1301 Howard is for end-of-line reductions and skate punk fashions.

The Wine Club

953 Harrison St at 6th ☎415/512-9086, ⓦwww.thewineclub.com. Huge warehouse space where the wine is offered at budget prices in torn cardboard boxes on the floor – tastings on Saturday afternoons.

Cafés

Brainwash

1122 Folsom St at 7th ☎415/861-FOOD, ⓦwww.brainwash.com. Gimmicky but fun: burgers, salads, and sandwiches are available while your laundry spins at the attached Laundromat. There's free live music most evenings.

Primo Patio

214 Townsend at 3rd ☎415/957-1129, ⓦwww.primopatiocafe.com. There's a massive covered patio hidden out back, dotted with multicolored umbrellas and old furniture. They serve sandwiches and burgers with a Brazilian or Caribbean twist, like jerk chicken and a Belize burrito, for less than $10.

Town's End

2 Townsend St at Embarcadero ☎415/512-0749. Gourmet brunch spot, famed for its tasty basket of baked goods that's served instead of bread. The food's

▼ LOST ART SALOON

modern American (rough-chopped smoked chicken hash, Cobb scramble with bacon and turkey), and most entrées cost $9.75–11.95.

Restaurants

Fringale

570 4th St at Brannan ☎415/543-0573, ⓦwww.fringalesf.com. Originally a Basque restaurant named for "the urge to eat" – think rustic recipes with plenty of Serrano ham and beans – this spot retained those touches on its menu, while adding wider-ranging French faves like duck confit.

The Public Restaurant and Bar

1489 Folsom St at 11th ☎415/552-3065, ⓦwww.thepublicsf.com. Decked out in eclectic thrift-store decor, this casual spot serves midprice modern American food. The two bars, thanks to live DJs and cheap happy-hour martinis, make it a good choice for hip, heavy-drinking dates.

Supperclub

657 Harrison St at 3rd ☎415/348-0900, ⓦwww.supperclub.com. Set in a baroque room fit to film a Warhol movie, this eatery has beds instead of seats (like every other branch of this global chainlet); servers are costumed like carnival performers (look for the waitress with the boa), and there's live, Cirque du Soleil–style entertainment while you eat. Set five-course meal is $60 ($70 Fri & Sat).

Thirsty Bear Brewing Company

661 Howard St at 2nd ☎415/974-0905, ⓦwww.thirstybear.com. Combination brewpub and tapas bar: don't let the dull name put you off the delicious food, like fluffy potato *croquetas* and crunchy fried calamari ($6–10 per plate). Packed in the evenings, when local workers go to drink and snack their cares away, it makes for an above-average lunch spot.

Tres Agaves

130 Townsend St at 2nd, ☎415/227-0500, ⓦwww.tresagave.com. Built in 1898 as a fire depot, this place now resembles a beer canteen in Tequila (the furniture's a direct replica). Sink shots or sip glasses of one of the hundreds of tequilas on sale here while catching a game at the bar, or slurp through reasonably priced Jalisco-region comfort food like crab broth with chile ancho and chipotle.

xyz

inside the *wHotel*, 181 3rd St at Howard ☎415/817-7836. Low-lit, sleek, and chic, this restaurant serves crisply prepared and well-presented dishes like fig wrapped in pancetta at expense-account prices. The bar is a preppy after-work scene.

Bars

111 Minna

111 Minna St at 2nd ☎415/974-1719, ⓦwww.111minnagallery.com. Stark, funky loft space that is a combination bar, art gallery, and performance space, usually with live DJs in the evening. The front room, with mismatched couches, is for chatting; it's more raucous in the rear by the tiny stage.

Asia SF

201 9th St at Howard ☎415/255-2742, ⓦwww.asiasf.com. Don't you dare call them drag queens

– the waitresses here are "gender illusionists" and perform campy burlesque on the bar throughout the evening. Try one of the delicious but deadly sake martinis.

Bacar Restaurant and Wine Salon

448 Brannan St at 4th ☏ 415/904-4100, ⓦ www.bacarsf.com. The loungey downstairs bar at this three-level restaurant is filled with overstuffed chairs where you can sample one of the hundred-plus wines served by the glass.

The Eagle Tavern

398 12th St at Harrison ☏ 415/626-0880, ⓦ www.sfeagle.com. Gay leather bar most popular on Sundays when it holds a late-afternoon "beer bust" for charity.

House of Shields

39 New Montgomery St at Mission ☏ 415/495-5436. Old-school, clubby piano bar, opened in 1908, that's preserved its long-term decor (dark wood paneling) and long-term regulars (slightly crumpled businessmen).

Loading Dock

1525 Mission St at 11th ☏ 415/864-1525, ⓦ www.loadingdocksf.com. This gay bar is fetish heaven, with a strict dress code of leather, uniform, or denim as well as an on-site playroom.

Loft 11

316 11th St at Folsom ☏ 415/701-8111, ⓦ www.loft11sf.com. Two-story swanky lounge with an electronica and chill out–centered playlist, as well as comfy, velvet-upholstered benches. Skip the so-so food and stick with the drinks.

Maxfield's

inside the *Palace Hotel*, 2 New Montgomery St at Market ☏ 415/392-8600. Mahogany-paneled, mural-decorated room that's a secluded and elegant place for a martini or two.

Mr. Smith's

34 Seventh St at Market ☏ 415/355-9991. Behind the signless, small door of this "speakeasy" lies chandeliers, exposed brick walls, and dark wood panels in the main room; there's a basement where DJs spin house and hip-hop on weekends.

Nihon Whisky Lounge

1779 Folsom St at 14th ☏ 415/551-4400, ⓦ www.nihon-sf.com. Japanese whisky lounge with more than 100 different brands, mostly Scottish as well as a handful of Japanese-made malts from Yamazaki. Snack on tasty Izakaya-style food (essentially Japanese tapas, like popcorn crab) with a mixed crowd of suited Nine to Fivers and rockers.

Powerhouse

1347 Folsom St at Doré ☏ 415/861-1790, ⓦ www.powerhouse-sf.com. One of the city's prime pickup joints, this gay bar has a strict dress code of uniform and leather – except on Thursday, which is underwear night. Free–$5.

Vino Venue

688 Mission St at Third ☏ 415/341-1930, ⓦ www.vinovenue.net. Gimmicky but fun: snag a stool, buy a card from the bartender, then insert it into one of the machines dotted around the place; it will then debit a given amount (from $1 to $6) for a single ounce shot.

Performing arts and film

Yerba Buena Center for the Arts

701 Mission St at 3rd ☎415/978-ARTS, ⓦwww.yerbabuenaarts.org. 750-seat theater hosting performances by prominent avant-garde dance, theater, and music companies now steered by visionary artistic director Ken Foster. $10 and up.

Metreon

101 4th St at Mission ☎415/537-3400, ⓦwww.metreon.com. The only megaplex within walking distance of downtown (at least until the San Francisco Centre opens), with fifteen screens of first-run movies.

Clubs and live music

330 Ritch Street

330 Ritch St at Townsend ☎415/541-9574. The only constant at this small, out-of-the-way club is its location: different nights attract wildly varied crowds, but it's best known for the Thursday Britpop Popscene party. $5–15.

Club Six

60 6th St at Market ☎415/863-1221. Mixed gay-straight club, with a program that focuses on trance and hardcore dance music. On one of the nastier blocks in town, so be careful as you arrive and leave. $5.

▼ CLUBS ON MARKET STREET

DNA Lounge

375 11th St at Harrison ☎415/626-1409, ⓦwww.dnalounge.com.
Downstairs is a large dance floor, while the mezzanine is a comfy, sofa-packed lounge where you can chill. $15–20.

Mezzanine

444 Jessie St at 5th ☎415/820-9669, ⓦwww.mezzaninesf.com. Massive megaclub with mainstream, brand-name DJs on weekends with an eclectic disco-to-electroclash playlist as well as live music on the new stage during the week. Make a reservation for the VIP Ultra Lounge if you're feeling flush and flash. No one arrives before midnight. $15.

SF Weekly Warfield

982 Market St at 6th ☎415/775-7722, ⓦwww.thefillmore.com/warfield.asp.
The Warfield is a beautiful, Art Deco music hall that was home to vaudeville headliners in the 1920s. It's now the setting for concerts by top-name touring bands as well as classic rock acts like the Pretenders; there's a smallish, intimate auditorium, with a dance floor on the first level and row seating on the second. The recent branded renaming was a deeply controversial move. $25 and up.

The Stud

399 9th St at Harrison ☎415/252-7883, ⓦwww.studsf.com. Legendary mixed/gay club that's still as popular as ever, attracting a diverse, energetic, and uninhibited crowd. Check out the fabulously freaky drag queen cabaret at "Trannyshack" on Tues. $5–10.

The Tenderloin and Civic Center

The Tenderloin has long been one of the shabbiest sections of town, overrun with flophouses and homeless vagrants. Local bureaucratic paralysis has continued to aggravate the problem, and the area's now rougher than ever – especially the stretch of Taylor Street around Turk and Eddy, where it's worth keeping your wits about you day or night. But waves of new Pakistani and South Asian immigrants are slowly improving the area, as well as establishing some excellent cheap eateries. Indeed, its budget eating and bar scenes are the big reasons to swing through here. Civic Center may at first seem a stark contrast to its grubby neighbor thanks to the grand Beaux Arts plaza, built after the 1906 disaster as architectural evidence of the city's fierce civic pride. Really, it's just the Tenderloin with better buildings, equally crammed with the homeless who camp out on the piazza.

Glide Memorial Church

330 Ellis St at Taylor ☎415/771-6300, ⓦwww.glide.org. Services Sun 9am & 11am. Part church, part social service provider for the local poor, Glide is best known for its rollicking 90-minute Sunday services, powered by a roof-raising gospel choir (it's well worth stopping by, but be sure to arrive at least an hour in advance to be sure of admission or you'll be stuck watching a live video feed of the fiesta in a side room). Whatever the day, step inside to see the AIDS Memorial Chapel, whose altarpiece triptych was the last work Keith Haring completed before his death from the disease.

Polk Gulch

Polk Gulch (Polk Street between O'Farrell and California) has long been the congregating point for the city's transgender community and a hub for the

▼ POLK GULCH

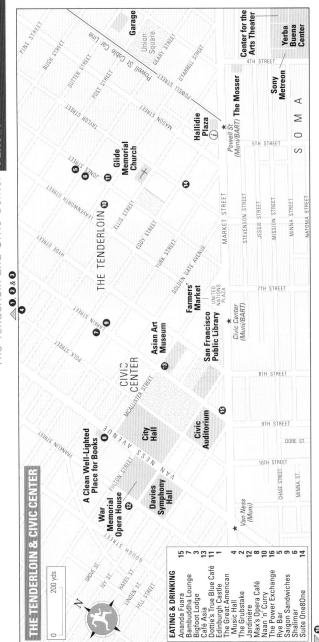

THE TENDERLOIN & CIVIC CENTER

EATING & DRINKING

Ananda Fuara	15
Bambuddha Lounge	7
Bigfoot Lodge	3
Café Asia	13
Dottie's True Blue Café	11
Edinburgh Castle	1
The Great American Music Hall	4
The Grubstake	2
Jardinière	12
Max's Opera Café	8
Naan 'n' Curry	10
The Power Exchange	16
Rye Bar	5
Saigon Sandwiches	9
Shalimar	6
Suite One80ne	14

Mayor Gavin Newsom

Telegenic and handsome local restaurateur **Gavin Newsom** easily won the 2004 mayoral election, then shoehorned himself onto the national stage by breaking California law to approve gay marriage certificates for more than 700 couples. His local popularity rose even further when he focused his attentions on social programs, rather than economic development, unlike his predecessor, larger-than-life Willie Brown. Newsom's committed to the "Care, not cash" initiative whereby welfare will not provide string-free support for the homeless; instead of a couple of hundred dollars doled out, no questions asked, each month, shelter and other in-kind support is available – provided someone can pass a drug test. It's too early to tell whether his plan will work, or not, though most locals are hopeful.

flesh trade; it was also home to several famous gay bars – though most of those bars, along with plenty of the hookers and rent boys, have now vanished. The one local landmark is the Mitchell Brothers' O'Farrell Theater at O'Farrell and Polk streets, the strip emporium once run by the pioneering pashas of porn, Artie and Jim Mitchell.

The brothers haven't been in charge for some years (Jim shot Artie in 1991), but it's one of the few remaining hubs for the local sex trade.

City Hall

Dr Carlton B. Goodlett Place at McAllister ☏415/554-4799, ⓦwww .sfgov.org/site/cityhall_index.asp. Mon–Fri 8am–8pm Tours Mon–Fri

▼ CITY HALL

10am, noon, 2pm. Free. The current City Hall dates from just after the 1906 fire, when local architects Bakewell and Brown won the contest to design a new building, submitting a sketch inspired by the haughty, gilded dome of Les Invalides in Paris, where both had studied. Costing a staggering $3.5 million to build, City Hall is conspicuously sumptuous throughout, especially the astonishingly detailed, carved Manchurian oak walls in the Board of Supervisors' Legislative Chamber. Recent earthquake retrofitting – which involved sliding giant ball bearings under its foundations – allows the entire structure to wobble more than two feet in either direction during a tremor. Although you can wander around the first floor of City Hall on your own, the best way to see the interior of the building is on one of the frequent free 45-minute tours that even include a whistlestop walk through the mayor's private office.

San Francisco Public Library

100 Larkin St at Grove ☎415/557-4400, ⓦsfpl.lib.ca.us/. Mon & Sat 10am–6pm, Tues–Thurs 9am–8pm, Fri noon–6pm, Sun noon–5pm. Free. The sleek library building that opened in 1996 – replacing the older one, which became the Asian Art Museum – was controversial from the start because though it had a large, bright central atrium and plenty of space for lounging readers, there just wasn't that much space for books; many volumes were simply sold off. The big draw here is the exhibition space–cum–reference library known as the James C. Hormel Gay and Lesbian Center, the first of its kind in the nation. Otherwise,

on the main floor, there are six Internet terminals that anyone can use free of charge for fifteen minutes, available on a first-come, first-served basis.

Asian Art Museum

200 Larkin St at Hyde ☎415/581-3500, ⓦwww.asianart.org. Tues–Wed & Fri–Sun 10am–5pm, Thurs 10am–9pm. $10, $5 after 5pm Thurs, free first Tues of every month. After the construction of the new public library, the old library's home, built in 1917, was sensitively converted to house the Asian Art Museum by Gae Aulenti, the same woman who turned a derelict train station in Paris into the fabulous Musée d'Orsay. She swept away the dark book stacks and opened up the interior to allow light to reach every corner, while still preserving details like the multicolored, ornamental ceiling decorations now visible in the upper galleries. The museum's holdings are vast, and it takes several hours to even hit just the highlights: the most famous treasure is probably the oldest known Chinese Buddha in the world, which dates back to 338 AD; there's also the wonderful wooden statue of Fudo Myoo, the wrathful Japanese god, with an expression more constipated than thunderous. Start browsing the holdings on the third floor and work down; there are free docent talks throughout the day, though it's better to skip the breathless, breakneck tours and stick with the audioguide.

Shops

A Clean, Well-Lighted Place for Books

Opera Plaza, 601 Van Ness Ave at Golden Gate ☎415/441-6670. The stock at this local favorite is now more

▲ SAN FRANCISCO PUBLIC LIBRARY

mainstream and less impressively exhaustive than it once was, but it's still worth checking out for the regular author readings – call for a schedule.

Heart of the City Farmers' Market

United Nations Plaza at Market St ☏415/558-9455. Sun 7am–5pm & Wed 7am–5.30pm. A good place for a cheap picnic lunch, especially given the low prices – just double-check the produce quality as it can be hit and miss.

Cafés and snacks

Ananda Fuara

1298 Market St at 9th ☏415/621-1994. Bargain vegetarian and vegan eatery with a vaguely cultish vibe: try the crunchy falafel or the impressive all-vegan mocha cake.

Café Asia

inside the Asian Art Museum, 200 Larkin St at Hyde ☏415/581-3630, ⍟www .asianart.org. Tues–Wed, Fri–Sun 10am–4.30pm, Thurs 10am–8.30pm. The museum café is finally open to hungry passersby who don't pay admission, serving superb Asian eats like a Korean pork sandwich with watercress or spicy salt and pepper fried chicken for $9 or so.

Dottie's True Blue Café

522 Jones St at O'Farrell ☏415/885-2767. Hefty portions of homemade cakes, eggs, and other breakfast favorites are the draw at this budget diner – plus its quirky owner, Kurt, who's always good for a gab. Try the whiskey fennel sausage scramble and save room for grilled corn bread. Breakfast and lunch only.

Saigon Sandwiches

560 Larkin St at Ellis ☏415/474-5698. Lunch only. Hole-in-the-wall store selling made-to-order Vietnamese sandwiches for $2 each – the BBQ pork is a standout.

Restaurants

The Grubstake

1525 Pine St at Polk ☏415/673-8268. Daily until 4am. Old-fashioned diner, housed in a decommissioned cable car, that serves all the basics for around $8 a dish, though the specialty is "The Nugget," a bacon cheeseburger topped with a fried egg.

Jardinière

300 Grove St at Franklin ☎415/861-5555, ⊛www.jardiniere.com. Indulge every culinary curiosity at this two-story rock-star restaurant – chef Traci des Jardins offers stunning, if pricey, French-Californian food (entrée prices hover around $30) like gnocchi with oxtail sauce in the exposed brick, low-lit space. Make sure to get a table upstairs away from the bar where the setting's more intimate.

Max's Opera Café

601 Van Ness Ave at Golden Gate ☎415/771-7300, ⊛www.maxsworld.com. Surprisingly good value given its location on the plaza (sandwiches $10-12), this old-school Jewish diner has leatherette chairs and green tables, old movie posters on the wall and a menu of staples like Philly cheesesteaks and matzo ball soup. The enormous bottomless sodas are a big plus.

Naan 'n Curry

478 O'Farrell St at Jones ☎415/775-1349. Shockingly low-cost Indian restaurant in the Tenderloin that's rundown, but clean, and serves mouth-tingling curries for only $5.99 or so; a chicken leg tandoori's a steal at $2.99. There are several other branches across the city.

Shalimar

532 Jones St at Geary ☎415/928-0333. Delicious, cheap Pakistani canteen-cum-café, where all the food is made to order before your eyes in the *kulcha* oven – the chicken tikka is a fantastic value at only $3.50.

Bars

Bambuddha

inside the *Phoenix Hotel*, 601 Eddy St at Larkin ☎415/885-5088, ⊛www.bambuddhalounge.com. Relaxed, groovy lounge, with a New Agey Asian vibe (think swirling, elemental decor and feng shui–favorable fountains).

Bigfoot Lodge

1750 Polk St at Washington ☎415/440-2355. Campy cocktail spot, themed as a 1950s ski lodge with plenty of faux wood, hunting trophies, antlers – as well as an enormous papier mâché statue of Bigfoot himself.

Edinburgh Castle

950 Geary St at Polk ☎415/885-4074, ⊛www.castlenews.com. Just your average Scottish bar filled with heraldic Highland memorabilia – even though it's actually run by Koreans. The pub food's worth sampling, especially their impressive fish-'n'-chips. Upstairs is a venue that hosts comedy and rock acts.

Rye Bar

688 Geary St at Leavenworth, ☎415/786-7803. Modern riff on a gentlemen's club – owned by the same couple as *A16* (see p.112) – with industrial, leathery decor, an antique pool table and a smoker's patio to boot. The menu's focused on cocktails and whiskeys – try the one of the muddled raspberry specials.

Performing arts and film

San Francisco Ballet and San Francisco Opera

War Memorial Opera House, 301 Van Ness Ave at Grove ☎ 415/864-3330, ⓦ www.sfballet.org & ⓦ www .sfopera.org. The third-oldest ballet company in the US (founded in 1933) remains in top form, thanks to artistic director Helgi Tomasson. Meanwhile, the opera – arguably the best in the country after New York's world-class Met – is known for its commitment to both avant-garde works and seat-filling crowd-pleasers; new artistic helmer David Gottlieb, fresh from a well-regarded stint running the Houston Opera, is likely to continue such eclectic programming. Ballet season runs from February to May; opera season is from September to December, with a short summer run June and July (call to check dates of the free simulcasts where performances are piped live to screens on Civic Plaza nearby) Ballet and opera tickets start from $25; the bargain option is standing in line for same-day standing tickets, available from 10am ($10–12, one per person).

San Francisco Symphony

Louise M. Davies Symphony Hall, 201 Van Ness Ave at Hayes ☎ 415/864-6000, ⓦ www.sfsymphony.org. Once-musty institution that's been catapulted to the first rank of American orchestras thanks to publicity hound and premier conductor Michael Tilson Thomas. Season runs from September through May,

with tickets starting at $25; $12 tickets for seats behind the stage are available two hours before performances.

Clubs and live music

The Great American Music Hall

859 O'Farrell St at Polk ☎ 415/885-0750, ⓦ www.musichallsf.com. Gorgeous, glamorous former bordello that plays host to a wide variety of rock, country, and world music acts. $10–20.

The Power Exchange

74 Otis St at Gough ☎ 415/487-9944, ⓦ www.powerexchange.com. Four-floor sexual playland, with themed rooms (leather, forest with tents, dance floor) and both gay and straight areas. Cover varies.

Suite One8One

181 Eddy St at Taylor ☎ 415/345-9900, ⓦ www.suite181.com. High-end hipster bar-club, with live DJs, billowing white curtains, and a comfy king-size bed as a rest from the dance floor. The heated outdoor patio's a major plus. $10 cover after 10pm.

▼ SUITE ONE8ONE

The Mission

The Mission District remains one of San Francisco's unmissable delights, even if there are few official sights to take in (with the exception of the old church here, which gave the neighborhood its name). Long a center of San Francisco's largely working-class Hispanic community, in the past decade this area's also absorbed waves of artsy Anglos, closely followed by cool-hunting dot-commandos, who drove rents to once unthinkable heights. Even so, the district retains its Latin roots, both in the hundreds of murals splashed everywhere and via its profusion of authentic Central and South American eateries. Indeed, the nightlife and restaurant scene here is one of the most vibrant (and well-priced) in the city; keep in mind that the area does still have its sketchy corners, especially at night, and there can be gang activity on Mission Street between Fourteenth and Nineteenth streets.

Dolores Park

One of the best greenspaces in the city, this park is like a splash of fresh air in the neighborhood, otherwise so dominated by gritty urban streets. Naturally,

▼ SUNBATHERS AT DOLORES PARK

Dolores Park is one of the best places to take advantage of the Mission's fog-free weather, with dozens of palm trees and rolling lawns spread over onto the side of a hill. The park's southwestern corner provides a spectacular view of the downtown skyline; on weekends, this chunk is known as Dolores Beach, as buff boys from the Castro come to bronze their gym-toned muscles.

Mission Dolores

3321 16th St at Dolores ☎415/621-8203, ⓦmissiondolores.citysearch.com. Basilica open daily 8am–noon, 1–4pm, old Mission open daily 9am–4pm. $3 suggested donation. The city's oldest building, a squat, white adobe that has weathered both of the city's major earthquakes and was named after the day European settlers set up camp here (the Friday of Sorrows, before Palm Sunday), dates back to 1791. The first Mass celebrated on the site, in a now-destroyed shack

▲ ❶, ❷ & ❸

THE MISSION

❹ ❺

14TH STREET

15TH   ❻ ❼

GUERRERO STREET ❽

VALENCIA STREET
JULIAN AVENUE
MISSION STREET
VAN NESS AVENUE
SHOTWELL STREET
FOLSOM STREET

LANDERS PLACE

Intersection for the Arts ❾

Clothes Contact ❿

16TH STREET

DOLORES STREET

Mission Dolores

Otsu **The Roxie Film Center** ⓫ ⓬

⓮
⓯
⓰
⓱

Hideo Wakamatsu

16TH STREET

HOFF ST.

⓭

17TH STREET

ALBION STREET

Good Vibrations ⓲

17TH STREET

CAPP STREET

⓳

⓴

18TH STREET

LINDA STREET
LAPIDGE ST.

㉑

Women's Building

CHURCH STREET

Dolores Park

19TH STREET

㉒

Dolores Beach

Dog Eared Books ㉔

20TH STREET

LIBERTY ST.

㉕

㉖

21ST STREET

Dema

HILL ST.

㉗
㉘ ㉙

Laku

㉚

22ND STREET

CAPP STREET
MISSION STREET
VAN NESS AVENUE
SHOTWELL STREET

SAN JOSE AVENUE
VALENCIA STREET

㉛

23RD STREET

㉜

24TH STREET

25TH STREET

N

0   600 yds

▷ Theater Artand

▷ ㉝

▷ Balmy Alley

EATING & DRINKING

Andalu	9
The Beauty Bar	22
Blondie's Bar & No Grill	16
Bombay Ice Creamery	15
Boogaloo's	28
Dalva	11
Delfina	21
Destino	3
Dosa	27
Elbo Room	18
El Farolito	32
Foreign Cinema	26
Hush Hush	4
La Cumbre	17
La Rondalla	24
Last Supper Club	31
Latin American Club	29
Luna Park	20
Martuni's	1
Medjool	25
Mighty	8
Pauline's	5
Pink	13
Radio Habana Social Club	30
Skylark	12
Sublounge	23
Tartine Bakery	19
Ti Couz	10
Walzwerk	6
We Be Sushi	14
Wilde Oscar's	7
Zeitgeist	2

constructed in 1776, marked the official founding of San Francisco. The Mission's interior is hushed and simple, with a hand-carved eighteenth-century Mexican altarpiece and floor plaques marking the burial sights

of prominent locals. The attached woody, overgrown cemetery is home to the unmarked graves of more than 5000 Native Americans and also holds the remains of several notable San Franciscans – note how many

▲ INTERIOR OF MISSION DOLORES

names on gravestones match street names across the city. The showy, tiered wedding cake of a basilica next door was added in 1913 and holds little of historic interest.

Women's Building

3543 18th St at Lapidge ☎ 415/431-1180, ⓦ www.womensbuilding .org. This community center hosts a variety of events and workshops, as well as a café, but is most notable for its exterior, tattooed with an enormous, sprawling mural known by the horrifically self-conscious name of *Maestrapeace*. On one side of the mural, there's an enormous mother-goddess figure, while on the other, oddly you'll find a gigantic portrait of Rigoberta Menchú, the Guatemalan woman who won the Nobel Peace Prize in 1992 - only to be later exposed as a James Frey–style fabulist.

Balmy Alley

Between Treat and Harrison streets, from 24th to 25th. There's barely an inch of wall in this small alleyway that isn't covered in one of the Mission's famed

murals; most are painted on wooden fences rather than stucco walls so they can be regularly replaced. Frankly, much of the artwork is more heartfelt than either skilled or beautiful, and the heavy-handed political imagery can be wearing; but the political themes do underscore how fiercely the Latin American heart of this neighborhood still thumps.

Valencia Street

This is the best place in the Mission to see how dynamically hip Anglo culture has fused with local Hispanic heritage – groovy boutiques and restaurants sit alongside age-old taquerias, and ambling down from 16th to 24th streets is a great way to spend an afternoon browsing and grazing.

Shops

Clothes Contact

473 Valencia St at 16th ☎ 415/621-3212. Secondhand clothing megaplex where you pay by the pound ($10), as weighed at checkout on a vintage scale – be prepared to rummage. Still one

of the best junk vintage stores in the city.

Dema

1038 Valencia St at 21st, Mission ☏415/206-0500, ⊛www.godemago.com. Feisty, brightly-colored women's clothing with plenty of op-arty prints and retro detailing, mostly designed by owner Dema Grim. T-shirts start around $30.

Dog Eared Books

900 Valencia St at 20th ☏415/282-1901, ⊛www.dogearedbooks.com. Smallish corner bookstore with a snappy selection of budget-priced remainders, as well as an eclectic range of secondhand titles, all in terrific condition.

Good Vibrations

603 Valencia St at 17th ☏415/522-5460, ⊛www.goodvibes.com. Gloriously sexy co-op store designed to destigmatize sex shops. It's packed with every imaginable sex toy, plus racks of erotica and candy store–style jars of condoms.

Hideo Wakamatsu

563 Valencia St at 17th ☏415/255-3029, ⊛www.hideostore.com. Only US outpost for this quirky Japanese luggage designer, who turns out leather satchels, carry-on wheelies and briefcases with offbeat touches – like the transparent plastic Skeleton.

Laku

1069 Valencia St at 22nd ☏415/695-1462, ⊛www.lakuyaeko.com. Handmade exquisite silk slippers by local designer Yaeko Yamashita. Also sells velvet hair accessories.

Otsu

3253 16th St at Dolores ☏415/255-7900 or 1-866/HEY-OTSU, ⊛www.veganmart.com. Closed Mon and Tues. Cruelty-free boutique, highlighting alternative materials including recycled tires and oilcloth for bags and belts, as well as a vast, impressive selection of shoes.

Cafés

Bombay Ice Creamery

552 Valencia St at 16th ☏415/431-1103. Tiny, authentic ice cream counter offers super-sweet, exotic flavors like cardamom and cashew-raisin.

Boogaloo's

3296 22nd St at Valencia ☏415/824-3211. Breakfast and lunch only. Bright orange and yellow walls perk up this basic café housed in an old drugstore, as does the hearty, Mex-inflected diner food; each dish costs around $5–7. There's plenty of veg-friendly options (expect fake steaks and tofu hash), but omnivores should definitely order anything made with chorizo (spicy sausage).

El Farolito

2779 Mission St at 24th ☏415/824-7877. A scruffy, 24-hour local institution, this Formica-table-crammed taqueria serves terrific food, most especially the *quesadilla suiza*, with chicken and cheese.

La Cumbre

515 Valencia St at 17th ☏415/863-8205. Old-fashioned taqueria with Wild West–inspired decor, staffed by chatty old women sharpening lethal carving knives before slicing meats to order. Budget $5 or so per person.

Pauline's

260 Valencia St at Brosnan ☏415/552-2050. Organic pizza joint that uses produce from its own

PLACES

The Mission

garden for its delicious whole pies – the pesto pizza is a house specialty.

Tartine Bakery

600 Guerrero St at 18th ℡415/487-2600. Tasty croissants, creamy cappuccinos, hearty crusty sandwiches, and wines by the glass at this gourmet bakery with huge shared tables and vases of fresh flowers wedged in the corners. There's no sign; just look for the green building and, usually, an enormous line on the sidewalk.

Restaurants

Andalu

3198 16th St at Guerrero ℡415/621-2211, ⓦwww.andalusf.com. Airy, upscale tapas bar serving a fusion menu of Californian, European, and comfort food – think ahi tartare tacos or mac 'n'-cheese – for $6–11 a dish.

Delfina

3621 18th St at Guerrero ℡415/552-4055. Groovy and great fun, this noisy, buzzy restaurant attracts everyone from grungy locals to visiting foodies – thanks to Cal-Ital dishes like ahi tuna with cannellini beans ($22). There's a cheaper pizzeria next door.

Destino

1815 Market St at Guerrero ℡415/552-4451, ⓦwww.destinosf.com. A small and welcoming restaurant, whose Peruvian chef-owner creates tasty, unexpected dishes like scallops in their shells coated in parmesan and juicy pork empanadas (large plates run $12-18). Wednesday's the night to come if you want to boogie, as there's tango dancing.

Dosa

995 Valencia St at 21st ℡415/642-3672, ⓦwww.dosasf.com. Throbbing South Indian space, with ochre walls and a Krishna statue overlooking the bar; squeeze into a table among the thirty-something diners and order dosas ($8–10.50) or uttapams ($9–11). The Chennai chicken appetizer ($8) and prawn masala curry main ($15) are outstanding.

Foreign Cinema

2534 Mission St at 21st ℡415/648-7600, ⓦwww.foreigncinema.com. Upscale Cal-French restaurant where movies are projected onto the large outdoor wall while you eat – though the delicious food's attraction enough, especially the oyster bar at brunch. The industrial-chic Laszlo martini bar next door, complete with DJ, is a place for after-dinner cocktails.

La Rondalla

901 Valencia St at 20th ℡415/647-7474. It's Christmas year-round at this Mexican dive, bedecked in tinsel and trinkets. The cheapish food's no better than average, but there's a handy takeout window and a full menu until 2am.

Last Supper Club

1199 Valencia St at 23rd ℡415/695-1199, ⓦwww.lastsupperclubsf.com. Rustic and rowdy Italian restaurant, with gilt mirrors and distressed walls: don't miss the garlicky, parmesan-laced pesto that's served with the bread, or the gnocchi with shredded venison. Mains run $17 or so; pastas cost $11–14.

Luna Park

694 Valencia St at 18th ℡415/553-8584, ⓦwww.lunaparksf.com.

Decked out like a lush bordello with deep red walls and ornamental chandeliers, this funky local favorite is always busy: the modern American entrées like pork cutlet with mushrooms and Gruyère or grilled half chicken cost around $16. Save room for the tableside s'mores and one of the tasty cocktails like a Granny Smith apple martini.

Radio Habana Social Club

1109 Valencia St at 22nd. No phone. Closed Sun. Quirky Cuban hole-in-the-wall, with tables jammed together and walls covered with picture frames and knicknacks. The food's cheap and tasty (tamales and empanadas for around $7), the crowd eclectic.

Ti Couz

3108 16th St at Valencia ☎415/252-7373. Friendly, hip crêperie that's consistently as one of the best restaurants around for this price range, serving pancakes for $6 or so.

Walzwerk

381 Van Ness Ave at 15th ☎415/551-7181, ⓦwww.walzwerk.com. Closed Mon. An East German eatery offering thumping, hearty comfort food like pork schnitzel and sweet cabbage for around $12–15 per dish. The decor's speakeasy-inspired (red velvet sofas and the like) with framed East German pop records on the wall.

We Be Sushi

538 Valencia St at 16th ☎415/565-0749. Although grungy and a little inauthentic, this remains an unmissable, well-loved local institution. You can gorge on cheap sushi (most is $2.50 for two pieces) while checking out what's on – the flyers on the

▲ RADIO HABANA SOCIAL CLUB

walls are great for up-to-date neighborhood listings.

Bars

The Beauty Bar

2299 Mission St at 19th ☎415/285-0323, ⓦwww.beautybar.com. Campy, tongue-in-cheek bar outfitted like a 1950s hair salon – all bubblegum pink colors and retro dryers. Most nights you can even enjoy a manicure with your cocktail.

Blondie's Bar & No Grill

540 Valencia St at 16th ☎415/864-2419, ⓦwww.blondiesbar.com. There's a wide selection of beers on tap at this local institution, which hosts a slightly older crowd and live music on its tiny stage. Smokers have their own cramped but handy room at the back.

Dalva

3121 16th St at Valencia ☎415/252-7740. Dark and divey wafer-thin space that's popular with a diverse, artsy crowd and often squeezes live bands and DJs into the slender front room.

Elbo Room

647 Valencia St at 17th ☎415/552-7788, ⓦwww.elbo.com. The onetime birthplace of acid jazz that's these days better known for its world music nights from dub and reggae to Afro-Cuban salsa or samba. Recommended. $6–10.

Latin American Club

3286 22nd St at Valencia ☎415/647-2732. Smallish bar with a pool table and walls covered in protest art; it's retained a neighborhood feel thanks to the reasonable prices.

Martuni's

4 Valencia St at Market ☎415/241-0205, ⓦwww.martunis.citysearch.com. Gay piano bar attracting a well-heeled, middle-aged crowd, all keen to sing along to classics from Judy, Liza, and Edith.

Medjool

above the *Elements Hostel*, 2522 Mission St at 21st ☎415/550-9055, ⓦwww.elementssf.com. The rooftop here, on top of a mid-range hostel (p.193), is a surprisingly buzzy nightspot serving drinks and Middle Eastern snacks on warm summer evenings.

Sublounge

620 20th St at 3rd ☎415/552-3603, ⓦwww.sublounge.com. Futuristic jet-set decor (airplane seats and video games) make this lounge one of the city's hotspots – not to mention the fact that it's smoker-friendly.

Wilde Oscar's

1900 Folsom St at 15th ☎415/621-7145. Gay pub decorated in an homage to the waggish wit,

with quotations all over the walls; there's an Irish-inflected bar-food menu, too.

Zeitgeist

199 Valencia St at Duboce ☎415/255-7505. Once-divey biker bar that's been given a faux grungy makeover by its new owners. Now, the large patio (terrific for smokers) is largely a haven for beer-swilling ironic hipsters here for the cheap drinks.

Performing arts and film

Intersection for the Arts

446 Valencia St at 16th ☎415/626-3311, ⓦwww.theintersection.org. Oldest alternative theater space in town, still churning out high-caliber political, community-oriented productions in a tiny venue. Ticket prices start at $9, with frequent "pay what you can" nights.

Roxie Film Center

3117 16th St at Valencia ☎415/863-1087, ⓦwww.roxie.com. Adventurous rep house and film distributor, often showcasing little-known documentaries or the work of first-time directors: there are two auditoria, a 275-seat theater and the 50-seat Little Roxie. It was recently bailed out financially by a local college and is set to start showing student films as part of the deal. Tickets are just $8.

Clubs and live music

Hush Hush

496 14th St at Guerrero ☎415/241-9944. Hidden , sign-less bar/club

that's nevertheless welcoming and friendly – whether you want to play pool or dance to retro cool music like nu disco or acid jazz with the slightly older crowd.

Mighty

119 Utah St at 15th ☎415/626-7001, ⓦwww.mightysf.com. Massive converted warehouse space – a combination art gallery, performance venue, club and lounge. As for the music, it's mostly live funk or DJs spinning old-school house. $10 and up.

Pink

2925 16th St at Capp ☎415/431-8889, ⓦwww.pinksf.com.

Candy-colored club that looks like a romance novelist's hideaway, with billowing curtains and candles. But this is a serious place to dance to deep house with a friendly, mixed gay-straight crowd. $5–10.

Skylark

3089 16th St at Valencia ☎415/621-9294, ⓦwww.skylarkbar.com. Yuppie-friendly hybrid club-bar, with low lighting and plenty of booths: there's a large dance floor and DJ booth at the back. More bar on weekdays, more club at weekends.

The Castro

West of the Mission lies Eureka Valley, or, as it's known around the world, the Castro. Claimed by San Francisco's gay community as it emerged as a group in the mid-1970s from the embers of Haight-Ashbury's hippie movement, the Castro quickly became synonymous with gay culture; it's one of the few places where straight people will find themselves in the minority. For such a lively and energetic area, there's oddly little here to see but rows of quaint houses and gay-friendly shops, but the out-and-proud vibe (not to mention some great restaurants) makes it a fun place to dawdle for an afternoon.

Harvey Milk Plaza

This plaza, on the corner of Castro and Market at the geographic heart of the city, was named in honor of San Francisco's first openly gay politician, who was murdered by Dan White, a jealous political rival, in 1978. In what became known as the "Twinkie defense," White claimed fast food additives had unbalanced his mind and so led him to shoot Milk; the judge clearly believed it since he only sentenced White to five years in jail. Today, Harvey Milk Plaza's a quiet place, home to a massive twenty-by-thirty-foot rainbow flag, the international symbol of gay pride that was first unfurled in San Francisco in the same year Milk died. Though it's sometimes used as a rallying point for protests, usually the plaza's oddly empty of people and acts mostly as a transit hub.

▼ RESIDENTIAL STREET IN THE CASTRO

Pink Triangle Park

Only dedicated in 2002, this monument (Ⓦwww .pinktrianglepark.net) is, astonishingly, the first in the country to be dedicated specifically to the gay victims of the Holocaust; it's wedged into the sliver of land between Seventeenth and Market streets. There's a pink triangle at its heart, filled with rough rose quartz shingle; around this, amid dozens of spiky cacti, fifteen pink triangle–topped granite columns poke through. Each represents 1000 men who were murdered by the Nazis because of their sexuality.

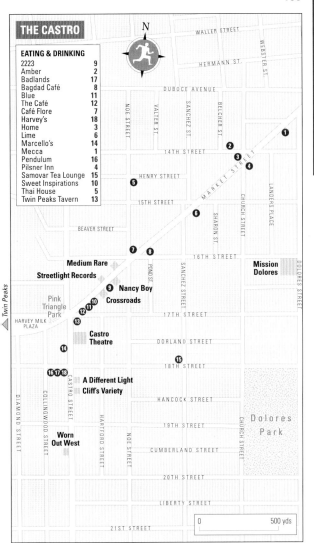

THE CASTRO

EATING & DRINKING

2223	9
Amber	2
Badlands	17
Bagdad Café	8
Blue	11
The Café	12
Café Flore	7
Harvey's	18
Home	3
Lime	6
Marcello's	14
Mecca	1
Pendulum	16
Pilsner Inn	4
Samovar Tea Lounge	15
Sweet Inspirations	10
Thai House	5
Twin Peaks Tavern	13

Castro Theatre

429 Castro St at Market ☎415/621-6120, ⓦwww.thecastrotheatre.com. $9. This old-school movie palace was built in 1922 and is a stunning example of the Mediterranean Revival style, its exterior marked out by lavish stucco decoration and knobbly, ornate windows. Inside's equally opulent, with foamy balconies and riotously over-the-top stucco ceilings. Also known as the Castro Cathedral, the theater

▲ THE CASTRO

PLACES

The Castro

Shops

Cliff's Variety

479 Castro St at 18th ☎415/431-5365, ⒲www.cliffsvariety.com. Twin-fronted, enormous emporium that's unique and endearing, stocking an only-in-the-Castro combo of home improvement essentials, kitschy homewares, and plenty of dress-up costumes (think boas by the yard). Unmissable.

Crossroads

2231 Market St at Noe ☎415/626-8989. Californian chainlet selling vintage clothes and remainders – it's not a steal, but it's worth checking for top-condition basics.

A Different Light

489 Castro St at 18th ☎415/431-0891, ⒲www.adlbooks.com. Well-stocked bookshop that features gay and lesbian titles – with an especially strong fiction section – and often hosts readings.

Medium Rare Music

2310 Market St at Noe ☎415/255-7273. Tiny, diva-heavy music

often hosts campy revivals of 1940s classics, playing to the most enthusiastic audience in town. Be sure to arrive early for pre-screening performances on the "mighty" Wurlitzer organ; the musical medley always draws to a close with Judy Garland's hit "San Francisco," with the crowd merrily clapping along.

The Castro: A brief history

Originally a working-class Irish neighborhood, no one can say definitively how or why **the Castro** ended up becoming the gayest neighborhood in the gayest city in the world. However, most historians point to the end of the hippie era, when the Haight-Ashbury flower children descended into heroin-addled mayhem, as the time when the Castro as we know it emerged. Disillusioned and politicized homosexuals – inspired by the Stonewall Riots in New York – left the Haight for this cheapie 'hood. They organized into social pressure groups as well as opening out-and-proud bars like the Pilsner Inn (see below); one of – their leaders, Harvey Milk, was elected to city government amid great fanfare – only to be assassinated in office a few years later. The Castro was heavily hit in the early 1980s by the arrival of HIV and AIDS; but thanks to Herculean efforts at prevention and treatment, infection rates have largely stabilized, although you'll still see ample evidence of AIDS-related events and leaflets anywhere you go in the Castro today.

▲ CASTRO THEATRE

store crammed with hi-NRG, Broadway, and cocktail lounge classics from Donna Summer to Peggy Lee.

Streetlight Records

2350 Market St at Noe ☎415/282-8000. A great selection of used records, tapes, and CDs. The perfect opportunity to beef up your collection on the cheap.

Worn Out West

582 Castro St at 19th ☎415/431-6020. Gay secondhand cowboy gear and leatherwear. Also worth checking for its wide selection of Western shirts.

Cafés

Bagdad Café

2295 Market St at 16th ☎415/621-4434. Most affordable 24-hour option in the neighborhood – like the diner food (sandwiches $6–8, omelettes $6.25–7.95) The decor is basic, but the prices make up for it. Cash only.

Café Flore

2298 Noe St at Market ☎415/621-8579. Cruisey café with a sunny, plant-filled courtyard that's a great place to grab a coffee and a gooey cake.

Marcello's

420 Castro St at 17th ☎415/863-3900. One of the top New York–style pizza joints in the city, serving pizza by the slice – it's especially known for its barbecue chicken–topped house special.

Samovar Tea Lounge

498 Sanchez St at 18th ☎415/626-4700, ⓦwww.samovartea.com. Earthy, cushion-filled café that serves more than 100 varieties of tea as well as tasty Asian snacks – curl up with a book for the afternoon in one of the overstuffed wicker chairs.

Sweet Inspirations

2239 Market St at Sanchez ☎415/621-8664. Open until 12.30am Fri & Sat. Tasty gourmet bakery with plenty of seating that serves dozens of different tarts and tortes – try a slice of the pear frangipane tart · as well as sandwiches and salads ($5.50–7.95). Refreshingly unfussy and uncruisey for its locale.

Restaurants

2223

2223 Market St at Noe ☎415/431-0692. This restaurant is one of the most mixed gay/straight venues in the neighborhood – likely because of its friendly, chatty vibe and because everyone wants to sample the sumptuous, simple interpretations of California cuisine like lightly roasted chicken topped with onion rings. The setting's a soft, pale yellow room with high ceilings and low lighting; expect to pay $18–20 an entrée.

Blue

2337 Market St at Castro ☎415/863-2583. Smallish retro restaurant decked out in industrial chromes and blacks and serving deliciously simple comfort food, like mac-'n'-cheese, homemade meatloaf, and chicken pot pie ($7.50–11.99), well into the early hours.

Home

2100 Market St at Church ☎415/503-0333. Home's popular with a mixed crowd of guppies and yuppies, thanks to its groovy patio bar and DJ. The food's reasonable (mostly $10–15 per entrée) and mostly comfort staples like *moules frites*.

Mecca

2029 Market at 14th ☎415/621-7000, ⊛ www.sfmecca.com. Impressive, if expensive, nightspot that's first and foremost an impressive eatery that offers trendy takes on Californian cuisine like saffron-braised monkfish ($28) and roasted pork tenderloin stuffed with tropical fruit ($24). It's also a great place for a cocktail (the vodka mojitos are oddly delicious), especially when there's cover-free live jazz – if you're a fan, try to snag one of the dinner tables that overlooks the small performance area by the massive central bar.

Thai House

151 Noe St at Henry ☎415/863-0374. Warm, intimate neighborhood eatery that looks incongruously like a Swiss chalet: the corn cakes are delicious, and the menu always offers quirky, tasty daily specials.

Bars

Amber

718 14th St at Market ☎415/626-7827. Mod bar, with retro mid-century fixtures, curtains made from dangling records, and old TVs. One of the few bars where smoking's permitted.

Badlands

4131 18th St at Castro ☎415/626-9320, ⊛www.sfbadlands.com. Video bar that attracts an attractive thirtysomething crowd. It's usually packed on weekends thanks to bargain specials like $1.25 bottled beer every Sunday 2–8pm.

Harvey's

500 Castro St at 18th ☎415/431-4278. Lively corner hotspot drawing a friendly gay crowd (and even the occasional lesbian), named in honor of Harvey Milk. Chug one of the specialty Bloody Marys: the Maria Callas, with vodka, tequila, and brandy, or the Mary Tyler Moore, with, ahem, more liquor and pepper vodka.

Lime

2247 Market St at Sanchez ☎415/621-5256. This mod spot is

more of a restaurant early in the evening before morphing into a mixed/gay club and bar later on. Try a coconut mojito ($8) or come for Sunday brunch for all-you-can-drink $6 mimosas.

Pendulum
4146 18th St at Castro ☎415/863-4441. Famous as the one place in the Castro that's popular among the black gay community; it's a low-key place to hang out, with pool tables and pinball, plus a smoker-friendly patio accessible via a smallish entrance in the back hallway.

Pilsner Inn
225 Church St at Market ☎415/621-7058. The best neighborhood gay bar in the Castro, filled with a diverse, slightly older crowd playing pool and darts; has a large, smoker-friendly patio out back.

Twin Peaks Tavern
401 Castro St at 17th ☎415/864-9470. Famous as the first gay bar in America to install transparent picture windows (rather than black them out). That happened in 1972; now it's filled with middle-class, older white men here to chat rather than listen to loud music.

Clubs and live music

The Café
2367 Market St at Castro ☎415/861-3846, ⓦwww.cafesf.com. One of the few places in the area with a DJ every night; music's mostly hi-NRG and house, and the dance floor's tiny, so be prepared to jostle the lesbians and swishy men who fill it most.

Haight-Ashbury and Hayes Valley

Haight-Ashbury lent its name to an entire era, giving the neighborhood a fame on which it has traded mercilessly ever since. Once a middle-class suburb with its own massive amusement park, the area hit hard times until the 1960s, when the students who had moved into the beautiful but battered Victorians were at the vanguard of the city's rebellious scene. Today it's theme-park boho, crammed with hippie-dippie souvenir shops. Best make your visit brief – unless you've a strong interest in tie-dyes and bongs – and continue on to the neighboring districts of Hayes Valley and the Lower Haight. You'll find much more interesting shopping, decent street life, and some lovely greenspaces as well. Make sure to wear comfy shoes as this is one of the hillier parts of town – bring a jacket, too, as fog can roll in suddenly on a summer day and blanket the area in chilly dampness.

Haight and Ashbury streets

It's surprising how unheralded this intersection, once the most famous street corner in the

▼ TIE-DYE SHOP ON HAIGHT STREET

world, is today. The only sign of its importance is the regular stream of tourists lining up to be photographed next to the street sign in homage to the Grateful Dead, who were snapped standing here in the 1960s and guaranteed that the words Haight and Ashbury were synonymous with free love and hippie values. As if to ram home the fact that the area's gung-ho glory days are long gone, there's now a branch of khaki-loving corporate clothier the Gap on the corner.

Grateful Dead house

710 Ashbury St at Waller. Much like the photogenic street sign on Haight Street, there's little to mark hippiedom's answer to Graceland, other than the clusters of people that sometimes gather here in pilgrimage. This old mansion was the band's home during the peak of its

Hippies in the Haight

The **hippie movement** began in the 1960s as an offshoot of the Beats and stressed Eastern religion and philosophy as well as pacifism, but as it matured, drugs – notably LSD, or acid, which wasn't illegal at the time – came to play a larger and larger role. The climax of this hippie revolution was 1967's Summer of Love, when more than 75,000 transitory residents called **Haight-Ashbury** home. Afterward, the mood in the Haight curdled, with heroin taking over as the drug of choice. It all burned out in the early 1970s, after which a splinter group of gay men – including hardcore hippie Harvey Milk – emerged, moved to the Castro, and founded the gay liberation movement.

fame from 1965 to 1969, and where they were photographed around the time of their notorious 1967 drug bust. Be aware that it's now a private home, so stay on the sidewalk.

The Lower Haight

The heavily wooded hilltop greenspace known as Buena Vista Park marks the unofficial divide between Haight-Ashbury and the area known as Lower Haight, which stretches along the main drag through to Fillmore Street. It's reassuringly free of both tourists and tie-dye T-shirt shops; instead you'll find record stores catering to local DJs at the forefront of the Bay Area club scene as well as a smattering of welcoming, locals-dominated bars and cafés.

Hayes Street

This thoroughfare, from Steiner to Van Ness, serves as the center for Hayes Valley, a chic, funky shopping district east of the Haight. It's lined with shady trees and sidewalk cafés, not to mention some of the coolest galleries and homeware and clothing stores around. In fact, the retail scene's so lively here that more and more stores are migrating to the area from the Castro, Union Square, and across the city, making

it hands-down one of the best places to shop or window shop in San Francisco.

Alamo Square

A manicured park perched on a hilltop, Alamo Square is most famous for the cluster of restored Victorians known as the "Painted Ladies," which overlook it from the east, at Steiner Street between Hayes and Grove. Built in 1894 and restored eighty years later in modern shades of hunter green, cream, and baby blue, the houses are unusual in that, although Italianate in style, they have gables – for more on Victorians' architecture, see p.100. And even if you've forgotten your camera, it's still worth the steep climb up here for the brilliant views across the city.

▼ "PAINTED LADIES", ALAMO SQUARE

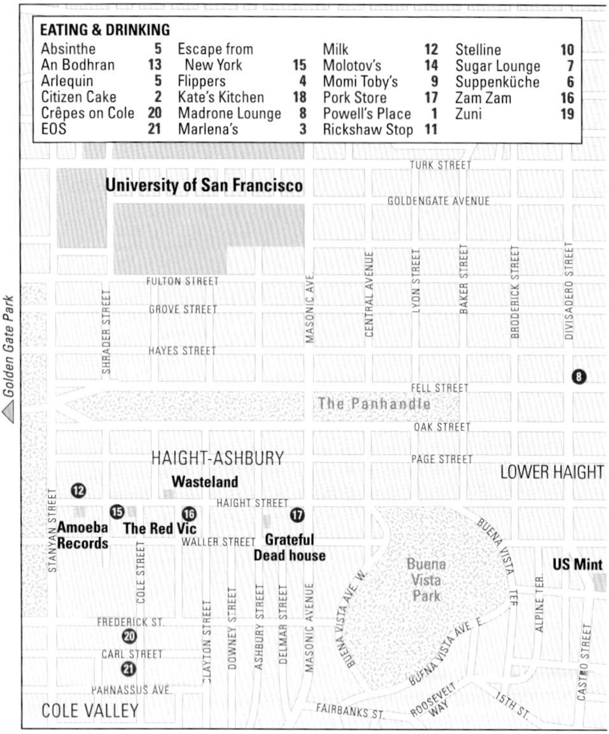

EATING & DRINKING
Absinthe 5
An Bodhran 13
Arlequin 5
Citizen Cake 2
Crêpes on Cole 20
EOS 21
Escape from New York 15
Flippers 4
Kate's Kitchen 18
Madrone Lounge 8
Marlena's 3
Milk 12
Molotov's 14
Momi Toby's 9
Pork Store 17
Powell's Place 1
Rickshaw Stop 11
Stelline 10
Sugar Lounge 7
Suppenküche 6
Zam Zam 16
Zuni 19
Golden Gate Park
University of San Francisco
TURK STREET
GOLDENGATE AVENUE
FULTON STREET
GROVE STREET
HAYES STREET
FELL STREET
OAK STREET
PAGE STREET
HAIGHT STREET
WALLER STREET
FREDERICK ST.
CARL STREET
PARNASSUS AVE.
FAIRBANKS ST.
SHRADER STREET
MASONIC AVE.
CENTRAL AVENUE
LYON STREET
BAKER STREET
BRODERICK STREET
DIVISADERO STREET
STANYAN STREET
COLE STREET
CLAYTON STREET
DOWNEY STREET
ASHBURY STREET
DELMAR STREET
MASONIC AVENUE
BUENA VISTA AVE. W.
BUENA VISTA TER.
BUENA VISTA AVE. E.
ALPINE TER.
CASTRO STREET
ROOSEVELT WAY
15TH ST.
The Panhandle
HAIGHT-ASHBURY
Wasteland
LOWER HAIGHT
Amoeba Records
The Red Vic
Grateful Dead house
Buena Vista Park
US Mint
COLE VALLEY

Shops

Amoeba Records

1855 Haight St at Stanyan ⓣ415/831-1200, ⓦwww.amoebamusic.com. One of the largest used-music retailers in America, offering a massive warehouse space filled with new and used CDs at bargain prices. Their original, somewhat bigger, location is in Berkeley (see p.169).

Azalea

411 Hayes St at Gough ⓣ415/861-9888, ⓦww.azaleasf.com. Terrific unisex boutique combining the best of womenswear (Habitual, LAMB, Sass & Bide) with cutting-edge men's lines like Josh Podoll and Corpus. There's also an onsite spa, Z Beauty Lounge, for mid-shop mani-pedis.

BPM

573 Hayes St at Laguna ⓣ415/487-8680. One of the top DJ record stores in the city, with the latest UK imports from top-name British DJs and masses of flyers for upcoming events.

Fabuloid

336 Hayes St at Franklin ⓣ415/355-0400, ⓦwww.fabuloid.com. Vintage, reworked vintage, and new clothes for men and women in a trippy, bubblegum-pink store. The in-house designs – made in

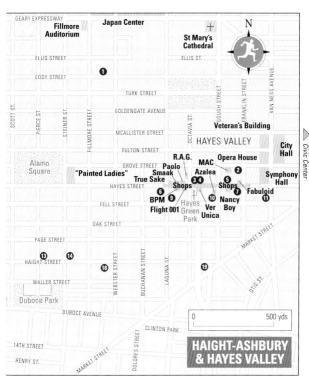

a workshop three blocks away – use ends of runs and dead-stock textiles for maximum retro effect.

Flight 001

525 Hayes St at Octavia ☎415/487-1001, ⓦwww.flight001.com. Sleek, futuristic travel store selling books, accessories, and dapper carry-on bags.

MAC (Modern Appeal Clothing)

387 Grove St at Gough ☎415/863-3011. Outstanding, directional local boutique (not to be confused with the makeup line), stocking European designers like Martin Margiela as well as local labels like Dema.

Nancy Boy

437 Hayes St at Gough ☎415/552-3802, ⓦwww.nancyboy.com. Kooky local cosmetics company, with the slogan "Tested on boyfriends, not on animals."

Paolo Iantorno

524 Hayes St at Laguna ☎415/552-4580, ⓦwww.paoloshoes.com. Local designer Paolo Iantorno is a little-known gem. He produces a limited edition (20–25 pairs) of his own fashion-forward men's and women's shoe designs in Italy, then sells them from his two stores in San Francisco for around $200.

▲ AMOEBA RECORDS

R.A.G.

541 Octavia St at Hayes ☎415/621-7718, ⓦwww.ragsf.com Closed Tues.
Innovative mini department store specializing in local designers under 30, who rent rack space to showcase their collections. Most things are surprisingly affordable, and the plus is that you'll never bump into anyone else wearing the same outfit.

Smaak

528 Hayes St at Octavia ☎415/503-1430, ⓔsmaaksf@yahoo.com.
All-Scandinavian clothing boutique, mostly women's with a smattering of men's gear like J. Lindeberg and Filippa K.

True Sake

560 Hayes St at Laguna ☎415/365-9555 or 1-800/949-3267, ⓦwww.truesake.com. A funky, all-sake store that sells more than 100 varieties. Each bottle is color-coded to show whether it's a light, crisp blend or a heftier, aged sake much like port.

Ver Unica

437b Hayes St at Gough ☎415/431-0688, ⓦwww.ver-unica.com.
Vintage shop selling high-grade secondhand clothing alongside a few brand-new retro-inspired pieces, mostly by local designers, like baby-soft cashmere underwear.

Wasteland

1660 Haight St at Belvedere ☎415/863-3150. Located in an old building that was once part of the amusement park that kick-started Haight-Ashbury, this store provides a high-end vintage selection, sorted by style and color.

Cafés and snacks

Arlequin

384b Hayes St at Gough ☎415/626-1211. Breakfast and lunch only.
Chichi patisserie with a subtle French accent, serving delicate breakfast pastries as well as lunchtime sandwiches for $6.50 or so (the pear, bacon, and white cheddar's a knockout) Make sure to head through the main café to the huge, secluded, flower-filled garden out back.

Citizen Cake

399 Grove St at Franklin ☎415/861-2228, ⊛www.citizencake.com.
Stylish, pricy café-bakery with a soft jazz soundtrack serving delectable, delicate pastries – its brunch specials, like eggy French toast with cocoa nib-banana butter and maple syrup ($9.50) or ham and roasted potato hash with poached eggs ($11), are unmissable. Pity about the snooty service, but brave it for the food.

Escape from New York

1737 Haight St at Shrader ☎415/668-5577. Low-key pizzeria decorated with old LPs that sells both whole pies and warmed-to-order slices with traditional toppings.

Flippers

482 Hayes St at Octavia ☎415/552-8880. Great-value brunches and gourmet hamburgers (try the teriyaki and pineapple); most of the huge portions cost just $8.75. There's ample outdoor seating.

Momi Toby's Revolution Café & Art Bar

528 Laguna St at Hayes ☎415/626-1508. The name may imply Che-level political fury, but the well-dressed, slouchy crowd is more groovy than guerrilla. Artful slackers linger over tasty bargain basics like a chicken-pesto focaccia sandwich (most $7.50).

Pork Store

1451 Haight St at Masonic ☎415/864-6981. Grimy, grungy hangout that's a good place to spot a smattering of locals amid the hordes of tourists on weekends. Brave the inevitable lines for hefty portions of brunch standbys like eggs and French toast ($7–9).

Restaurants

Crêpes on Cole

100 Carl St at Cole ☎415/664-1800. The crêpes here are filling, inventive, and enormous – and most cost only $6.95 or so. Even better, every serving comes piled high with home fries.

EOS

901 Cole St at Carl ☎415/566-3063. The spectacular East–West fusion food, like ginger Caesar salad or lemongrass risotto, is expensive but unmissable at this neighborhood favorite; there's a wine bar with a snack menu attached if you don't want to splash out the money for a proper meal.

Kate's Kitchen

471 Haight St at Fillmore ☎415/626-3984. Monstrously huge portions of hearty breakfast food and crunchy hush puppies are the pluses at this small diner, as are the under-$8 budget prices; the massive crowds on weekends are the minus.

Powell's Place

1521 Eddy St at Fillmore ☎415/409-1338. Onetime Hayes Valley staple driven out by the high rents, but thankfully just as noteworthy in its new location. The house specialty is Southern fried chicken ($12), and every dinner is served with couple of crumbly corn muffins.

Stelline

330 Gough St at Hayes ☎415/626-4292. Red-checkered tablecloths, a handwritten and photocopied menu, plus affable, chatty staff make this a standout among the cheap cafés nearby; entrées cost $8.

Suppenküche

601 Hayes St at Laguna ☎415/252-9289, ⓦwww.suppenkuche.com. Dinner only; Sunday brunch. There's a beer-hall atmosphere at this German eatery, complete with bare walls and stark pine chairs and tables; entrées like Wiener schnitzel cost $16–22.

Zuni

1658 Market St at Gough ☎415/552-2522. Once nouveau and now a staple, Zuni features the most famous Caesar salad in town – made with home-cured anchovies – and an equally legendary focaccia hamburger made in a rustic Californian style; most entrées are in the $18–22 range. The minimalist, rather nineties decor is heavy on brick and glass.

Bars

Absinthe

398 Hayes St at Gough ☎415/551-1590. The bar of this plush, velvet-draped brasserie-bistro is a handy option in the area, since it's open until 2am and serves smallish snacks for $6 or so per plate. Best option for grazing is one of the cheese selections – $5 per chunk – paired with a glass of whatever the sommelier suggests.

An Bodhran

688 Haight St at Pierce, ☎415/431-4724. Pick of the cluster of Irish pubs on this strip, with occasional live Irish folk music plus Wednesday quiz night.

Marlena's

488 Hayes St at Octavia ☎415/864-6672. Old-school drag bar serving cheap drinks to a thirty- and fortysomething crowd of men and a few women.

Molotov's

582 Haight St at Steiner ☎415/558-8019. One of the few places nearby still catering for rockers rather than clubbers, with the major plus of plenty of seating.

Rickshaw Stop

155 Fell St at Franklin ☎415/861-2011, ⓦwww.rickshawstop.com. Cavernous and intriguing neighborhood bar swathed in red velvet and furnished with thrift store pieces. It's

▼ DINING ALFRESCO AT *ABSINTHE*

known for its offbeat music programming (with free live performances most nights), arty lit-geek crowd, and friendly vibe.

Sugar Lounge

377 Hayes St at Gough ☎415/255-7144. Sugar-rimmed cocktails – hence the name – served in a sleek, slim space with mid-tempo music and a dressy thirtysomething crowd.

Zam Zam

1663 Haight St at Clayton ☎415/861-2545. The retro jazz jukebox sets the tone at this casbah-style cocktail lounge – the music's loungy and low key, as is the vibe. The bar was once run by a notoriously finicky owner; after his death, the place was bought by a group of his regulars, who preserved its old-fashioned ambience.

Performing arts and film

The Red Vic

1727 Haight St at Cole ☎415/668-3994, ⓦwww.redvicmoviehouse.com. Grab a wooden bowl of popcorn and a beer or glass of wine, then kick your feet up on the benches at this friendly cinematic collective where cult faves predominate.

Clubs and live music

Madrone Lounge

500 Divisadero St at Fell ☎415/241-0202, ⓦwww.madronelounge.com. Club–cum–art lounge with bimonthly art exhibits, live music from homegrown bands every Wednesday, and DJs or a vintage jukebox other nights. Order a cocktail made with one of the bar's home-infused vodkas.

Milk

1840 Haight St at Stanyan ☎415/387-6455. Superb DJ bar and lounge with white booths as well as posh drinks, and one of the best rosters of music in the city – cutting-edge DJs spinning house and, at weekends, reggae. Cover $3–10; free before 9pm.

Golden Gate Park

Spreading three miles or so west from Haight-Ashbury, rolling, rustic Golden Gate Park is the lungs of the city; a visit here is essential to understanding the outdoorsiness so central to the local character. Designed in 1871 by William Hall to mimic the style of Central Park creator Frederick Law Olmsted, the park (daily dawn–dusk; for schedules and tour information call ☏415/263-0991 or 415/750-5442) has more than a thousand acres of gardens and forest. The original plan was to keep the park free of buildings, but that proved impossible after the 1894 World's Fair was held here: the exhibition's legacy is the two major museums in the park's eastern end. And if you get lost on the spaghetti-like tangled walkways, don't worry – it's intentional; from the outset, Golden Gate was to be a woodland park, and so the streets were artfully curved to encourage promenading. Today, it's hugely popular with locals for that very reason – they can jog along the park's paths or spend an afternoon picnicking here.

de Young Museum & California Academy of Sciences

50 Tea Garden Drive ☏415/863-3330, ⓦwww.deyoungmuseum.org. Tues–Thurs, Sat & Sunday 9.30am–5.15pm, Fri 9.30am–8.45pm, $10 with additional charge (varies) for special exhibitions, free first Tues of each month, $2 discount daily with valid Muni transfer. The park's museum hub has been the site of major

▼ THE DE YOUNG MUSEUM

construction for several years: at the time of this writing, the original home of the California Academy of Sciences is still being gutted and reconstructed as a state-of-the-art facility by Renzo Piano scheduled for a 2008 debut – for a review of its temporary home in SoMa, see p.116. In the meantime, visitors will have to make do with the truly showstopping new de Young museum, which reopened in October 2005. Its formerly cramped, Neoclassical quarters have been replaced with a futuristic, copper-plated building by Herzog and de Meuron; the finish should blend with the surrounding plants as it develops a greenish patina with age.

The museum has two parts: the twisty tower offers no art but plenty of views, though the tiny elevators, which cause a bottleneck at its base, are a major design flaw; note that it closes 45 minutes before the rest of the building. Then there's the exhibition space, which underscores how schizophrenic and catch-all the museum's holdings now are, with a confusing layout that blurs unrelated art together – Mesoamerican figurines, for example, segue inexplicably into modernist sculpture. The onetime backbones of the de Young, Oceanic and African art, are now stuck in a corner; of its foregrounded western holdings,

look for lots of splotchy Diebenkorns and Mary Cassatt's tender Impressionist portrait of her mother, as well as Josiah McElheny's dazzling handblown silver glass sculpture. Overall, the displays disappoint severely in comparison with their jaw-dropping new home.

Japanese Tea Garden

415/752-4227, www.frp .org/japanese_tea_garden.asp. Daily 8.30am–6pm. $3.50. One of the best-known attractions in the park, this Asian fantasy of miniature trees and groomed plants was actually created for the 1894 Exposition by an Australian, George Turner Marsh, who had lived in Japan; and it was only once Marsh sold it soon after to the park's commissioners that a Japanese man took charge. A massive bronze Buddha cast in 1790 dominates the twisty, nook-crammed garden; make sure to climb the humpback bridge and check out the magnificent but careworn pagoda from San Francisco's Panama Pacific International Exhibition in 1915. The best time to enjoy the garden's tranquility is when it first opens, before the busloads of tourists start pouring in. If you're peckish and want to nibble on some cookies and sip a cup of tea, you'll need to fork over an additional $2.95.

Good fortune

The **fortune cookie** is certainly a California creation, but the arguments over whether it's Japanese or Chinese still rage. The most popular story of its invention involves Makota Hagiwara, the first Japanese owner of the Tea Garden. In 1907 (or so the story goes) Hagiwara was ousted from his job there by racist mayor James Phelan. Amid much protest, Hagiwara was quickly reinstated and invented the cookies as a way of delivering thank-you notes to those friends who'd championed his cause.

GOLDEN GATE PARK

CABRILLO STREET

N

25TH AVENUE

FULTON STREET

Buffalo
Paddock

Spreckels
Lake

Golden Gate Park

CROSS OVER DRIVE

CHAIN OF LAKES DRIVE

JOHN F KENNEDY DRIVE

Golden Gate
Park
Stadium

MIDDLE DRIVE

MARTIN LUTHER KING JR DRIVE

1

25TH
AVE

23RD
AVE

Murphy Windmill | Dutch Windmill
& Beach Chalet

0   800 yds

Conservatory of Flowers

☏415/831-2700, ⓦwww
.conservatoryofflowers.org. Tues–Sun
9.30am–4.30pm, $5. The redwood
and glass building that houses
the Conservatory of Flowers is
a spectacular sight, supposedly
modeled after the Palm House
at London's Kew Gardens,

▼ PAGODA IN THE JAPANESE TEA GARDEN

though in fact it looks nothing
like it. In fact, the building,
with its whitewashed wooden
frame, resembles the overblown
greenhouse of a well-to-do
Victorian country home.
Its spiffy appearance hides a
troubled history: it was closed
in 1995 after severe storm
damage rocked the building,
necessitating the plants' being
shipped to local nurseries while
the ailing conservatory was
shored up. After eight years and
$25 million worth of renovation
and restoration, the conservatory
finally reopened in Sept 2003.
Now it's divided into five
sections: a temporary exhibition
space, a room filled with
Victorian-style potted plants,
lowland and highland tropics
areas (in the latter, look for the
spindly orchids from the Andes),
and best of all, a cool, aquatic
plant room that showcases its
showstoppingly huge Victoria
waterlilies.

San Francisco Botanical
Garden at Strybing
Arboretum

☏415/661-1316, ⓦwww.
sfbotanicalgarden.org. Mon–Fri
8am–4.30pm, Sat–Sun & holidays
10am–5pm, tours daily at 1.30pm.
Free. This 75-acre botanical

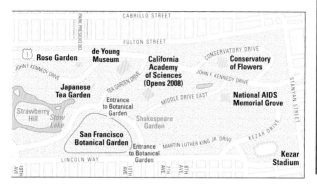

garden is home to more than 7000 varieties of plants, with its miniature gardens focusing on plants from different regions of the world – desert to tropical; especially appealing is the headily scented garden of fragrance. The main entrance is at Ninth Avenue and Lincoln Way on the park's southern edge.

National AIDS Memorial Grove

℡ 415/750-8340, ⓦ www. aidsmemorial.org. Set up in 1998, this seven-acre memorial garden was the first of its kind in the country, designed to commemorate those who died of AIDS-related illnesses and provide a serene place where loved ones could linger. Rocks with single names dot the edge of the large oval greenspace and, though a little rundown these days, it's astonishingly peaceful.

Shakespeare Garden

This tiny, hedged garden, centered on an old-fashioned sundial and dotted with benches, showcases every flower and plant mentioned in Shakespeare's works, whether plays, sonnets, or poems. There's a metal plaque full of the relevant quotes on a brick wall at the edge of the lawn.

The Windmills

ⓦ www.goldengateparkwindmills. org. On the western edge of the park stand twin windmills. The 1902 **Dutch Windmill** to the north, which once pumped water to a reservoir in the park, was carefully restored to working order in the 1980s. To the south is the now sail-less **Murphy Windmill**, which was built three years later and long

▼ THE DUTCH WINDMILL

▲ THE BUFFALO PADDOCK

lagged several years behind in restoration; funds have finally been raised to renovate it, though there's no firm date yet for the sails to start turning again.

Buffalo Paddock

No one can say exactly why there's a small herd of bison in the park, but they're certainly a daunting and impressive sight – the best place to get close to them is in their feeding area at the far west end of the paddock.

Beach Chalet

1000 Great Highway ☎415-751-2766. This two-story, white-pillared building houses a series of 1930s frescoes depicting the growth of the city of San Francisco, as well as a park visitor center. Upstairs is the lively *Beach Chalet Brewery and Restaurant* (☎415/386-8439, Ⓦwww.beachchalet.com), a great place to grab a late weekend brunch; try the crab omelette and a pint of the Beach Blanket Blond Ale.

The Richmond and the Sunset

On the western edge of San Francisco, flanking Golden Gate Park, are two flat, fog-choked districts that are rarely on visitors' itineraries: the Richmond to the north and the southern Sunset. It's a shame, as there's plenty to see, including the California Palace of the Legion of Honor, which has a fair claim to being the best museum in the city. More than anything, though, both neighborhoods are refreshingly ordinary in comparison to the self-consciously visitor-friendly sites downtown. The Richmond's often referred to as the "new Chinatown," due to the Chinese residents who've thronged there in recent years, but it's also appealing for its handy beaches. The Sunset is more residential, with swaths of identical postwar stucco houses, but nevertheless has quite a thriving niche of stores and restaurants huddled around the junction of Ninth Avenue and Irving Street.

Clement Street

This commercial drag is the hub of the thriving Chinese community that's flocked to the Richmond District in recent years. Between Park Presidio and Arguello boulevards, the shop fronts are filled with dim sum stores, eat-in restaurants, and Chinese groceries, which makes for an atmospheric, authentically Asian way to spend a hungry afternoon.

▼ MARKET ON CLEMENT STREET

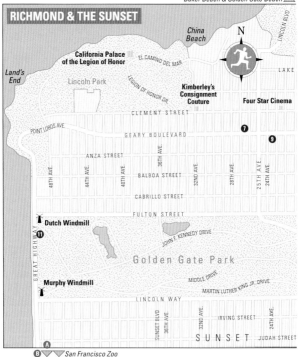

RICHMOND & THE SUNSET

China Beach

N

LINCOLN BLVD

California Palace
of the Legion of Honor

EL CAMINO DEL MAR

Land's
End

Lincoln Park

LEGION OF HONOR DR

Kimberley's
Consignment
Couture

LAKE

Four Star Cinema

CLEMENT STREET

POINT LOBOS AVE

GEARY BOULEVARD

❼

❾

ANZA STREET

36TH AVE

48TH AVE

44TH AVE

40TH AVE

BALBOA STREET

32ND AVE

28TH AVE

25TH AVE

24TH AVE

CABRILLO STREET

FULTON STREET

Dutch Windmill

GREAT HIGHWAY

❶❶

JOHN F. KENNEDY DRIVE

Golden Gate Park

Murphy Windmill

MIDDLE DRIVE

MARTIN LUTHER KING JR. DRIVE

LINCOLN WAY

SUNSET BLVD

36TH AVE

32ND AVE

IRVING STREET

24TH AVE

S U N S E T

JUDAH STREET

Ⓐ
Ⓑ ▽▽ *San Francisco Zoo*

California Palace of the Legion of Honor

inside Lincoln Park ☎ 415/863-3330, ⊛ www.legionofhonor.org. Tues–Sun 9.30am–5pm. $10, $2 reduction with valid Muni transfer, free first Tues of every month. Built on a cliff-side hilltop in 1920 by Alma de Bretteville (see p.69) to resemble the Legion d'Honneur in Paris, this museum is an elegant Neoclassical building centered on a pillared courtyard. It houses Alma's staggering collection of works by the sensual French sculptor Rodin, which is more than reason enough to make the journey here. There are more than eighty pieces, including bronzes, maquettes, and marble sculptures: standouts include *Fallen Angel*, *The Athlete*, and a small preparatory study for *The Kiss*. There's even an original cast of *The Thinker* (actually intended to be the writer Dante) in the main courtyard outside. The Rodin holdings at this magnificent museum are somewhat let down by the other collections, including a lackluster set of Old Masters; even so, look for a typically distorted, graphic novel–style canvas of John the Baptist by El Greco and some fine English portraiture by Raeburn and Gainsborough. The basement space is used for a rotating display of touring shows that vary wildly in quality.

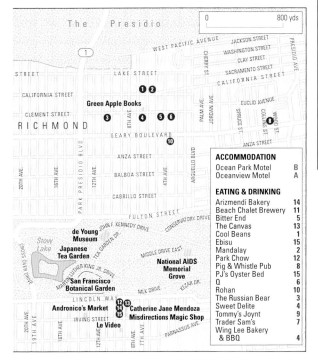

Lincoln Park and Land's End

The Legion of Honor is surrounded by **Lincoln Park**, a craggy but beautiful greenspace carved into the coast at the northwesternmost tip of the city. There are several trails curving around the cliffs here that make for a pleasant hike, and it's worth trekking around to the section known as **Land's End**, one of the few true wilderness areas left in the city. Littering the base of its jagged cliffs are the broken hulls of ships that have failed to navigate the violent currents here; with luck, at low tide you can see chunks of the wooden wreckage. If you stay until dusk, there are spectacular views of the Golden Gate Bridge and Marin headlands.

Baker, China, and Golden Gate beaches

Baker Beach is the most popular of the three, with wide, clean swaths of sand and easy access by Muni bus (#29) or car (there's ample street parking nearby). However, **China Beach** immediately to its south – reachable via a cluster of rocks at low tide – is more sheltered and has better facilities, including showers. **Golden Gate Beach** to the north is a predominantly gay and nude beach, and quite tricky to reach, via a series of perilous trails; if you do make it, one reward is a stunning view of the Golden Gate Bridge. Note that though all three beaches here may be inviting,

▲ THE HOLOCAUST MEMORIAL AT THE LEGION OF HONOR

the water is bone-chillingly cold and the currents fierce, so don't plan more than a quick paddle.

Cliff House

1090 Point Lobos Rd ☎ 415/386-3300, ⓦ www.cliffhouse.com. Though it may be hard to imagine, the Cliff House, which now houses a pair of so-so restaurants, was the centerpiece of the Fisherman's Wharf of the nineteenth century. The brainchild of mining millionaire (and later mayor of San Francisco) Adolph Sutro, the complex contained rides and sideshows, as well as ocean-fed pools that could accommodate 25,000 swimmers at a time. The owners of the house's current, architecturally-challenged incarnation (several previous versions burned down) attempted to spiff it up via exhaustive upgrades

in 2004. The redo resulted in *Sutro's*, a swanky but unremarkable restaurant, and The Bistro, an all-day dining room that's equally skippable. Renovations aside, the reason to stop by isn't the bland, modern American food, it's the restaurant's stunning location with views along the cliffs that overlook the Pacific Ocean.

San Francisco Zoo

Sloat Boulevard at 47th Ave, Sunset ☎ 415/753-7080, ⓦ www.sfzoo .org. Daily 10am–5pm. $10, free first Wed of each month. At time of writing, the zoo is close to the end of a multiyear, multimillion-dollar project to replace all its old-fashioned enclosures with natural habitats, like the new the Lemur Forest, a lush park home to a crowd of rare lemurs from Madagascar, and the three-acre African Savanna for giraffes, zebras, ostriches and others. The great apes' current concrete homes will have been replaced by a massive forest by early 2007. In the meantime, make sure to check out the new Children's Zoo, with its beautifully restored,

▼ OCEAN BEACH

▲ CLIFF HOUSE

old-fashioned carousel ($2) and charming Penguin Island, where the colony of chatty, highly sociable birds is fed every day at 3pm (2.30pm on Thurs).

Shops

Andronico's Market

1200 Irving St at 14th, Sunset ⓣ415/661-3220. California's gourmet answer to Safeway, with pricey but gorgeous produce that's great to grab for a picnic lunch in the park, plus microbrew beers and a fine wine selection.

Catherine Jane Mendoza

1234 9th Ave at Lincoln, Sunset ⓣ415/464-1855, ⓦwww .catherinejane.net. Slim-fit girly clothes with a ruffly, Nicole Miller–esque style from this local designer.

Green Apple Books

506 Clement St at 6th, Richmond ⓣ415/387-2272, ⓦwww .greenapplebooks.com. Funky, browsable store with deft, eccentric touches like the

regular section of "Books That Will Never Be Oprah's Picks."

Kimberley's Consignment Couture

3020 Clement St at 32nd, Richmond ⓣ415/752-2223. Closed Sun & Mon. Ultra-high-end castoffs from denizens of the tony mansions nearby – expect last season's gently worn Prada at 75 percent off.

Misdirections Magic Shop

1236 9th Ave at Irving, Sunset ⓣ415/566-2180, ⓦwww .misdirections.com. Stash a bunny in your hat and stroll over to this magic megastore, stocking every trick from card and coin sleights-of-hand to levitation aids.

Le Video

1231 9th Ave at Irving ⓣ415/566-3606, ⓦwww.levideo.com. Gaudy-fronted store – there's an enormous film reel swirling on its frontage – that contains the most comprehensive collection of videos in the country, with both domestic and imported rarities.

Cafés

Arizmendi Bakery

1331 9th Ave at Irving, Sunset ℡415/566-3117, Ⓦwww .arizmendibakery.com. Closed Mon. Worker-owned co-op bakery that envelopes the sidewalk with the scent of fresh-baked loaves: duck inside to pick through the cabinet of breads, muffins, and cakes, or try the daily pizza special, like tomatoes with marinated artichoke hearts ($2 slice, $8 half, $16 whole).

The Canvas

1200 9th Ave at Lincoln Way, Sunset ℡415/504-0060, Ⓦwww .thecanvasgallery.com. Massive café-cum-gallery-cum-performance space cluttered with mismatched mod furniture and rattan sofas;

▼ COOL BEANS

sandwiches like pesto grilled cheese cost $6.50 or so. There are performances each night: Monday is poetry, Wednesday open mic, Thursday through Saturday live jazz and rock (free–$5).

Cool Beans

4342 California St at 6th, Richmond ℡415/750-1955. This brightly painted neighborhood coffeehouse is a charming hippie throwback, with star- and flower-shaped tables, plus board games to play. Sandwiches like lox and cream cheese or salami, pesto, and sundried tomato cost $5.

Sweet Delite

519 Clement St at 6th, Richmond ℡415/386-8222. First, gawk at the racks and racks of Chinese and American candies in plastic boxes here, then gorge on a bag of exotic sweets. There's also an ice cream bar that serves creamy, scented tapioca ball tea.

Wing Lee Bakery & BBQ

503 Clement St at 6th, Richmond ℡415/668-9481. No-nonsense Chinese dim sum store where there's little English spoken and you can gorge on pearlescent peanut dumplings for a couple of bucks.

Restaurants

Ebisu

1283 9th Ave at Irving, Sunset ℡415/566-1700. There are two rooms at this mid-priced eatery: one has a sushi bar, the other is a traditional Japanese-style restaurant complete with tatami mats. Aside from a fantastic sushi selection (considered one of the best in town), the vegetarian options are good, as are the super-crunchy tempura dishes.

Mandalay

4348 California St at 5th, Richmond ☎415/386-3895. Even if the decor at this budget Burmese restaurant is a little bland, the food is anything but – some of their more notable specials, scrawled on the chalkboard out front, include green papaya salad and remarkable homemade tofu dishes. Budget $12 a head.

Park Chow

1240 9th Ave at Lincoln, Sunset ☎415/665-9912. Solid, consistent renditions of pizzas, pastas, and the like, perfect for a post-park lunch. Expect sandwiches ($7.95–8.95) and Italian classics like eggplant parmesan ($9.50).

PJ's Oyster Bed

737 Irving St at 9th, Sunset ☎415/566-7775, ⊛www .pjsoysterbed.com. Dinner only. This rowdy, unpretentious restaurant offers spicy, tangy Cajun dishes such as jambalaya and blackened catfish for around $18 or so a dish, as well as "Creole tapas" snacks like Louisiana blue crab cakes for $12. Whatever the day, watch for the free vodka Jell-O shots that the owner passes out.

Q

225 Clement St at 3rd, Richmond ☎415/752-2298. This hipster outpost in the Richmond is an over-the-top diner, with funky features like a booth at the back where a tree grows through the table. Portions are huge, and the menu's mostly comfort food, like Southern fried chicken and

beer-battered catfish for $10 or so a head.

Rohan

3809 Geary Blvd at 2nd, Richmond ☎415/221-5095, ⊛www.rohanlounge. com. Closed Mon. Funky lounge and bar, swathed in taffeta curtains, serving contemporary twists on Korean cuisine – grills are only $8.75–11.50 – until 1.30am at weekends. The soju cocktails are killer.

The Russian Bear

939 Clement St at 10th, Richmond ☎415/752-8197 Russian restaurant popular with expats thanks to its traditional dishes like borscht and veal – the decor is mind-boggling, with seemingly every surface mirrored or covered in gilt.

Tommy's Joynt

5929 Geary Blvd at 23rd, Richmond ☎415/387-4747 ⊛www.tommysjoynt .com. Most people come for the enchiladas at this homey, low-cost Mexican restaurant. It's energetic and supercrowded whatever day or time, and is known for its exhaustive selection of obscure tequilas. Budget $20 for dinner and drinks.

Bars

Bitter End

441 Clement St at 5th, Richmond ☎415/221-9538. The youngest and hippest of the Irish bars on the main Richmond drag, notable for its cozy fireplace and impressive selection of whiskeys.

Pig & Whistle Pub

2801 Geary Blvd at Wood, Richmond ☎415/885-4779. A thoroughly British pub, serving a good selection of English and

Californian microbrews. There's a dartboard and jukebox crammed with Brit-rock classics.

Trader Sam's

6150 Geary Blvd at 26th, Richmond ☏415/221-0773. Open since 1939, this is a classic Tiki bar, complete with flaming bowls of exotically named cocktails – try a P38 cocktail, served in a salad bowl with four straws.

Performing arts and film

The Four Star

2200 Clement St at 23rd, Richmond ☏415/666-3488, ⓦwww.hkinsf .com. Funky Richmond theater screening a mix of art films and Hong Kong action flicks for the local Asian community.

Berkeley

A fifteen-minute BART ride brings you to the East Bay, home to two wildly different cities, Oakland (see p.172) and Berkeley. Notorious as a hippie haven and antiwar hotspot in the 1960s, Berkeley today retains the friendly, unflappable vibe that Haight-Ashbury has long lost. This is mostly due to the massive university that dominates the town – a fact underscored by the hordes of bobbing backpacks that fill its streets and cafés every weekday. But you don't have to be politically radical to come here: this city was also where the light, ingredient-driven cooking style known as California cuisine was first invented (indeed, the area around the first Cal-cuisine eatery, *Chez Panisse*, has been dubbed the Gourmet Ghetto). It's also a feast for readers – Telegraph Avenue, downtown's main shopping drag, is lined with bookstores, where you can easily spend an entire day browsing for hard-to-find first editions or trashy pulp paperbacks.

Telegraph Avenue

Telegraph Avenue is the commercial strip of town and the best place to start exploring. Its amenities are tailored to service the adjacent campus, so it's filled with bargain sandwich stores and takeout restaurants as well as terrific record and bookshops – the blocks running south of campus to Alcatraz Avenue are an especially bustling place to browse (see pp.169–171 for listings). It's appealing enough at any time, but only on a weekday lunchtime can you truly gauge how much the hordes of students drive the surrounding town's economy.

▼ STUDENT LIFE ON TELEGRAPH AVENUE

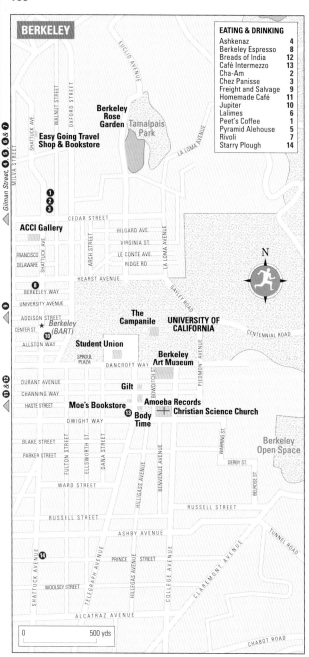

BERKELEY

◁ Gilman Street ❹ ❺ ❻ & ❼
◁ ❾
◁ ❶❶ & ❶❷

EATING & DRINKING

Ashkenaz	4
Berkeley Espresso	8
Breads of India	12
Café Intermezzo	13
Cha-Am	2
Chez Panisse	3
Freight and Salvage	9
Homemade Café	11
Jupiter	10
Lalimes	6
Peet's Coffee	1
Pyramid Alehouse	5
Rivoli	7
Starry Plough	14

EUCLID AVENUE

WALNUT STREET
OXFORD STREET
MILVA STREET

Berkeley Rose Garden
Tamalpais Park

LA LOMA AVENUE

Easy Going Travel Shop & Bookstore

SHATTUCK AVE.
MILVA STREET

❶
❷
❸

CEDAR STREET

ACCI Gallery

ARCH STREET
HILGARD AVE.
VIRGINIA ST.
LE CONTE AVE.
RIDGE RD

LA LOMA AVENUE

FRANCISCO
DELAWARE

SHATTUCK AVE.

HEARST AVENUE

GAYLEY ROAD

N

❽ BERKELEY WAY
UNIVERSITY AVENUE

ADDISON STREET
CENTER ST. ★ **Berkeley (BART)**
❿ ALLSTON WAY

The Campanile

UNIVERSITY OF CALIFORNIA

CENTENNIAL ROAD

Student Union
SPROUL PLAZA
BANCROFT WAY

Berkeley Art Museum

PIEDMON AVENUE

BOWDITCH ST.

DURANT AVENUE
CHANNING WAY
HASTE STREET

Gilt

Moe's Bookstore **Amoeba Records**
❸ ✝ **Christian Science Church**
Body Time

WARRING ST.

Berkeley Open Space

DWIGHT WAY

BLAKE STREET
PARKER STREET

FULTON STREET
ELLSWORTH ST.
DANA STREET

HILLGASS AVENUE
BENVENUE AVENUE

DERBY ST.
BELROSE ST.

WARD STREET

RUSSELL STREET

RUSSELL STREET

ASHBY AVENUE

TUNNEL ROAD

❶❹

SHATTUCK AVENUE

PRINCE STREET
WOOLSEY STREET

TELEGRAPH AVENUE
HILLEGAS AVENUE
COLLEGE AVENUE
CLAREMONT AVENUE

ALCATRAZ AVENUE

CHABOT ROAD

0	500 yds

UC-Berkeley campus

℡510/642-5215, ⓦwww.berkeley
.edu. 90min tours Mon–Sat 10am, Sun
1pm. Free. Founded in 1873 on
a former cow pasture by high-
minded refugee academics from
the East Coast, the university (as
well as the city) was named to
honor Irish bishop/philosopher/
poet George Berkeley, whose
lines "Westward the course of
the empire takes its way" so
inspired the founders. Its half-
mile square main campus is so
bucolic and tree-crammed that
it looks like a forest onto which
a university has been forcibly
grafted, the large Neoclassical
buildings jutting out suddenly
from behind leafy copses. And
despite such on-campus quirks
as the Free Speech Movement
Café, the student body here
is oddly normal-looking
when compared to the hippie
stereotype Berkeley is often
associated with.

If you choose not to take one
of the chatty, free tours, you can
stroll the campus on your own
following Strawberry Creek,
the path running off southeast
from the main entry on West
Entrance Road. It leads through
the greenery to Sproul Plaza,
the campus's largest public
space, usually lined with tables
shilling student societies or the
clink and bong of Hare Krishna
converts.

Though the cynical might
be tempted to sneer at
the university's supposed
idealism, it's impossible not
to warm to the place while
walking around here; and it's
worth remembering that the
university's hippie reputation
often obscures its superb
scholarly record. This is where
plutonium was discovered
in 1941, and the element
berkelium was first isolated by
Berkeley-based boffins (hence
the name). Just remember, if
you want to sound like a local,
don't shorthand to Berkeley
– call it UC or Cal. The best
way to explore is to wander
around the campus, though
we've picked out two highlights
below; another place to check
out is the university's Botanical
Garden (daily 9am–5pm, 7pm
in summer; free) on the hillier,
eastern edge of the campus,
thirty lushly-landscaped acres of
cacti and plants.

PLACES Berkeley

▼ THE BERKELEY-SATHER GATE

Campanile

☎510/642-5215, ⓦwww.berkeley
.edu/visitors/campanile.html. Mon–Fri
10am–4pm, Sat 10am–5pm, Sun
10am–1.30pm & 3–5pm; $2. Like
a monochrome replica of
the clocktower in Venice's St.
Mark's Square, the Sather Tower
(its official name) was put
up in 1917, using more than
500 tons of structural steel to
cross-brace the building and
secure it against tremors. It's
poorly located at the rear of
the campus, resulting in hit-
and-miss views, especially if
the Bay is fogbound – though
on most days, you should be
able to pick out the cone of
the Transamerica Pyramid (see
p.70); what's most surprising is
how much less green and rural
Berkeley's campus looks from
on high. The less mobile should
note that there's a long elevator
ride, then a narrow stairway, to
reach the top.

Berkeley Art Museum

2626 Bancroft Way at College
☎510/642-0808, ⓦwww.bampfa
.berkeley.edu. Wed, Fri–Sun 11am–
5pm, Thurs 11am–7pm; $8, free first
Thurs of each month. A Modernist,
angular building that stands out
amid the twee Neoclassicism

elsewhere on campus, the
museum houses both a selection
of European greatest hits from
Rubens to Picasso as well as a
stunning roundup of works by
1950s American favorite Hans
Hofmann. There are almost fifty
of his canvases here spanning
his entire career, from early
figurative works like *Japanese
Girl* to later, daubed abstracts
such as *Indian Summer*. Check
the museum's website for up-
to-date info on its impressive
and often controversial roster of
traveling exhibits as well as for
updates on its plans to move to
a new location, near the western
gate, sometime in the next
couple of years.

First Church of Christ Scientist

2619 Dwight Way at
Bowditch ☎510/845-7199,
ⓦwww.1stchurchberkeley.org.
Built in the Craftsman style
with a few Gothic touches,
this handsome church looks
like a collision of Swiss chalets,
squished together to form a
single building, their individual
roofs jutting out in odd places
from the final structure. The
architect was Bernard Maybeck,
the same man behind the

▼ FIRST CHURCH OF CHRIST SCIENTIST

mournful and equally detailed Palace of Fine Arts in the Presidio (see p.107). The church is laid out in a Greek Cross floor plan and spanned by a massive redwood truss, with carved neo-Gothic tracery and Byzantine-inspired painted decoration. The only public tours take place on the first Sunday of every month, starting at 12.15pm (ⓦwww .friendsoffirstchurch.org), but if you're in town at other times, you're always welcome to attend services (Sun 11am, Wed 8pm).

Shops

Amoeba Records

2455 Telegraph Ave ☎510/549-1125, ⓦwww.amoebamusic.com. Though the branch in Haight-Ashbury is handier, this is the original site of the Bay Area's best secondhand record shop and it shows. The selection's bigger and the staff even nerdier, so you'll likely be able to find almost any CD you want, no matter how obscure it may be. It's also worth stopping by to pick up the flyers advertising cheap local gigs.

Body Time

2509 Telegraph Ave ☎510/548-3686, ⓦwww.bodytime.com. Although this Bay Area–born company sold its original name to the UK-based Body Shop, it still puts out a full range of aromatic natural bath oils, shampoos, and skin creams and offers soaps by the slice and custom-scented lotions.

Cody's Books

1730 4th St ☎510/559-9500, ⓦwww .codysbooks.com. Acknowledged for its size and selection as the highest profile of the numerous local booksellers, specializing in fiction, poetry, and literary criticism.

Easy Going Travel Shop & Bookstore

1385 Shattuck Ave ☎510/843-3533, ⓦwww.easygoing.com. Packed with travel paraphernalia, offering a wide selection of guidebooks and maps as well as regular travel-writer appearances.

Moe's Bookstore

2476 Telegraph Ave ☎510/849-2087, ⓦwww.moesbooks.com. Vast four-story new and used bookstore, renowned for its art section on the top floor.

Cafés

Berkeley Espresso

1900 Shattuck Ave at Hearst ☎510/848-9576. Relaxed and less overrun by students than other cafés, this large, loungeable place, dotted with blond wood chairs and rickety tables, offers free wireless Internet access and serious doorstep-sized sandwiches.

Café Intermezzo

2442 Telegraph Ave at Haste ☎510/849-4592. Come to this café for huge sandwiches on homemade bread (many of them $5 or less), plus great coffee and enormous salads, slathered in one of its house-mixed dressings.

Homemade Café

2454 Sacramento St at Dwight ☎510/845-1940. Breakfast and lunch only. If you want a hearty breakfast, there's nowhere better in town – though expect to share a table when at peak hours as it's a tiny space. There are some Jewish touches, like cheese blintzes, among the traditional offerings, as well as a few Mexican accents – the Home Fry Heaven is potatoes smothered in cheese, salsa, sour cream, and guacamole.

Peet's Coffee

2124 Vine St at Walnut ☎510/841-0564, ⓦwww.peets.com. The cutesy West Coast chain of coffeehouses started with this original branch, which opened in 1966.

Restaurants

Breads of India

2448 Sacramento St at Dwight ☎510/848-7684. Leave lots of room for the breads, a specialty at this tasty but cramped Indian lunch spot. Budget $10 a head and you'll be stuffed.

Cha-Am

1543 Shattuck Ave at Cedar ☎510/848-9664. Climb the stairs up to this always crowded budget restaurant, tucked away in the upscale Gourmet Ghetto, for deliciously spicy Thai food at bargain prices like grilled salmon in tamarind sauce or pad Thai (both $6.95).

Chez Panisse

1517 Shattuck Ave at Cedar ☎510/548-5525, ⓦwww.chezpanisse.com. Closed Sun. First and still the best of the modern Californian cuisineries, overseen by legendary chef Alice Waters. Dinner's served at two sittings, 6pm and 8.30pm, with a prix fixe menu that costs $50–85 depending on the night of the week. Some of the delights served here include Dungeness crab and petrale sole ravioli with chervil and chives and a Bosc pear cornmeal *crostata* with vin santo ice cream. Reservations essential. There's a slightly more

modestly priced café upstairs for à la carte lunches and dinners.

Lalimes

1329 Gilman St at Peralta ☎510/527-9838, ⓦwww.lalimes.com. Unofficially known as "Chez Panisse for locals," this is another upscale gourmet outpost that offers an outstanding take on California cuisine in a low-key setting (mains $23–27). The à la carte menu changes monthly, to allow for seasonal specials, though asparagus in prosciutto with shaved Parmesan ($9.75) and triple almond tart with almond ice cream ($7.50) are both sumptuous staples. Make sure to book well in advance – it's full every night of the week.

Rivoli

1539 Solano Ave at Peralta ☎510/526-2542, ⓦwww.rivolirestaurant.com. The atmosphere at this low-lit Mediterranean restaurant is casual but friendly. Though the intriguing menu (entrées run $18–22.50) changes every three weeks, three signature dishes always remain – a hot fudge sundae ($6.95), a Caesar salad ($8.95), and the true standout, tender portobello mushroom fritters with lemon aioli ($9.50).

Bars

Jupiter

2181 Shattuck Ave at Center ☎510/843-8277, ⓦwww.jupiterbeer.com. This bar has a multitude of beers, live jazz on weekends, and an outdoor beer garden. The decor has a distinctly German Gothic vibe, from the seats made from church pews to the large chandeliers.

Pyramid Alehouse

901 Gilman St at 8th ☏510/528-9880,
ⓦ www.pyramidbrew.com. Great
microbrewed beers – try the
Hefeweizen – in a popular pub,
a brightly lit, loft-style space
with ample seating. There are
tours of the on-site brewery
(Mon–Fri 5.30pm, Sat & Sun 2
& 4pm).

Starry Plough

3101 Shattuck Ave at Prince
☏510/841-2082, ⓦwww
.starryploughpub.com. Convivial
Irish bar with bargain-priced
live rock and country many
evenings and a handy dartboard.

Clubs and live music

Ashkenaz

1317 San Pablo Ave ☏510/525-5054,
ⓦ www.ashkenaz.com. World music
and dance café that presents acts
ranging from modern Afrobeat
to the best of the Balkans.
Cover $7–10.

Freight and Salvage

1111 Addison St ☏510/548-1761,
ⓦ www.thefreight.org. Founded
in 1968, this coffeehouse-style
venue is a nonprofit dedicated
to preserving and promoting
traditional music (whether
blues, jazz, or folk), and its
usual lineup leans heavily on
singer-songwriters. Cover
$4.50–20.50.

Gilman Street

924 Gilman St ☏510/525-9926,
ⓦ www.924gilman.org. Better
known as the Gilman, or the
Alternative Music Foundation,
this nonprofit punk landmark
is an indie mainstay booking
emerging bands and often
propelling them to stardom
(Green Day and Rancid
rocked out here). $7 per show
plus $2 compulsory annual
membership.

Oakland

Oakland's unfairly ignored by visitors – and it's true that there's little at first glance to lure them here from across the bay. Look closer, though and you'll see – aside from the determinedly sunny weather, a sharp contrast to the foggy city – there are pockets of intriguing history. Take the prettified streets of Old Oakland, for example, whose Victorian-era brick architecture showcases what San Francisco would look like today were it not for the tragedy of the 1906 earthquake and fire. Downtown's streets can still seem oddly lifeless outside office hours, but the city's slowly being transformed by a dual transfusion of new residents: lesbians siphoned from the hipster swarms of the Mission and Castro and resilient dot-commers still slaving in Silicon Valley but keen to snap up bargain housing.

Chinatown

bounded by Broadway, Alice, 13th, and 7th streets. In comparison with San Francisco's bustling, throbbing Chinatown, the Oakland enclave is oddly empty of people: there are few trinket stores, and most of the shop fronts are filled with Vietnamese or Chinese supermarkets, which spill fragrant produce onto the sidewalk. It's only during the last weekend of August that the streets really come to life, when the Chinatown StreetFest (℡510/893-8979, Ⓦwww.oaklandchinatownstreetfest.com) brings out performers, stalls, and the crowds.

Old Oakland

bounded by Broadway, Clay, 11th, and 8th streets Ⓦwww.oldoakland.org. Dating back to the 1870s, this district – the East Bay's answer to San Francisco's Jackson Square – holds a superb collection of grand old Victorian commercial architecture that's worth exploring even if modern restoration has left it feeling a little too manicured with uniform signage and flawless cream and gilt paintwork. Most of the storefronts are home to attorneys or interior design firms so there are few places to browse, though there's an excellent Farmers' Market every Friday from 9am to 2pm. The liveliest area, filled with one-off stores and cafés, is at the corner of Washington and Eighth streets.

Jack London Square

Embarcadero and Broadway ℡510/814-6000, Ⓦwww.jacklondonsquare.com. Named

▼ STATUE OF JACK LONDON

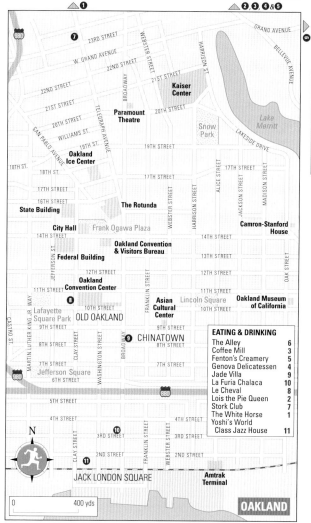

EATING & DRINKING

The Alley	6
Coffee Mill	3
Fenton's Creamery	5
Genova Delicatessen	4
Jade Villa	9
La Furia Chalaca	10
Le Cheval	8
Lois the Pie Queen	2
Stork Club	7
The White Horse	1
Yoshi's World Class Jazz House	11

OAKLAND

after hometown hero Jack London, this waterfront mall complex is anchored by a massive Barnes and Noble and filled with unremarkable brand-name eateries like *TGI Friday's* and *Tony Roma's*. Its only lures are its fine waterfront location, and the fact that there are fewer souvenir hawkers and less tourist tackiness than at Fisherman's Wharf. London completists should grab a pint at *Heinold's First and Last Chance Saloon*, a tiny bar built in 1883 from the hull of a whaling ship where

London actually drank – note the slanted door that's never been fixed since it skewed in the wake of the 1906 earthquake. The other appealing draw here is *Yoshi's*, a first-rate jazz club.

Paramount Theatre

2025 Broadway at 20th ☎510/893-2300 or 510/465-6400, ⓦwww .paramounttheatre.com. $1 for 2-hour tour, first and third Sat of each month at 10am. Built by the same architect as the ornate, Mediterranean Revival Castro Theatre (see p.139), this imposing landmark, with its Egyptian-inspired, mosaic-clad facade, is a streamlined Art Deco masterpiece from 1931. It's worth trying to catch one of the infrequent tours of the building, or even stopping by for a movie (complete with Wurlitzer organ), so you can see the elaborate, mosaic- and relief-studded interior; the hodgepodge of styles is a result of the large number of artists hired to help decorate it. The Paramount

also hosts live shows and stage spectaculars.

Oakland Museum of California

1000 Oak St at 10th ☎510/238-2200 or 1-888/625-6873, ⓦwww. museumca.org. Wed–Sat 10am–5pm, Sun noon–5pm, first Fri of each month 10am–9pm. $8, free second Sun of each month. This museum's housed in a stark and impressive modernist building designed by legendary architect Kevin Roche (one of the team behind the fabled TWA terminal at New York's JFK airport). Architectural value aside, the views across the city and the Bay from the rooftop sculpture garden are stunning. As for its holdings, they're smartly curated in three distinct sections, one per floor: California Ecology simulates the state's diverse climates from seaside to mountaintop, while California History ranges from early Native American settlement to the modern day. The best section, though, is undoubtedly the top floor, which showcases a collection of California arts, including some fine examples of turn-of-the-century Arts & Crafts furniture. The museum's scheduled renovations – mostly a buffing-up of the interior gallery spaces – have been delayed and at time of writing are set to begin in 2007 and last for two years or so. Call to check for updates if you're making a special journey.

Cafés and snacks

Coffee Mill

3363 Grand Ave at Elwood ☎510/465-4224. This café doubles as an art

▼ PARAMOUNT THEATRE

The Black Panthers

Formed amidst the poverty of West Oakland in 1966 by black-rights activists Huey Newton and Bobby Seale, the leather-jacket- and beret-sporting members of the **Black Panther Party for Self-Defense** captured the media spotlight with their militant rhetoric and occasional gun battles with police.

Mixing socialism with black pride, the Panthers developed "survival programs" in black communities that included the establishment of free medical clinics. But infighting took a heavy toll, and when Newton fled to Cuba in 1974 to avoid prosecution for drug use, a cascading series of resignations led to the group's disbanding by the end of the decade. Former Panther David Hilliard conducts Black Panther Legacy Tours (☏ 510/986-0660, ⓦ www.blackpanthertours.com; $25) through the Huey P. Newton Foundation on the last Saturday of each month. Tours depart at noon at the West Oakland Public Library on West 18 Street.

gallery and often hosts poetry readings, too.

Fenton's Creamery

4226 Piedmont Ave at Ridgeway ☏ 510/658-7000, ⓦ www .fentonscreamery.com. The ultimate old-style ice cream parlor serving sundaes, fries, and burgers or sandwiches ($5.25–12.95).

Genova Delicatessen

5095 Telegraph Ave at 51st ☏ 510/652-7401. Friendly deli, decked with hanging sausages, that serves amazing sandwiches for around $5.

Restaurants

Le Cheval

1007 Clay St at 10th ☏ 510/763-8495. A moderately priced Vietnamese restaurant, serving simple food in chic, spacious surroundings.

La Furia Chalaca

310 Broadway at 3rd ☏ 510/451-4206. Lively Peruvian seafood spot, serving well-priced pastas ($10–14) as well as traditional dishes like chili and lime-drenched ceviche ($13) and fried breaded fish steak served with heaps of shrimp and shellfish ($14).

Jade Villa

800 Broadway at 8th ☏ 510/839-1688. One of the best places to sample dim sum or Cantonese cuisine in Chinatown at fair prices.

Lois the Pie Queen

851 60th St at Adeline ☏ 510/658-5616. Locally legendary for its Southern-style sweet potato pies, this cozy diner serves hearty breakfasts and dinners for less than $10.

Bars

The Alley

3325 Grand Ave at Santa Clara ☏ 510/444-8505. Closed Mon. A piano bar where locals come specifically to sing – given the boozy conviviality and the right melody, you will too.

Stork Club

2330 Telegraph Ave at 23rd ☏ 510/444-6174, ⓦ www .storkcluboakland.com. Closed Mon. On the main road toward the UC- Berkeley campus, this historic club is presently a favorite with DJs and indie bands. Cover $5 and up.

The White Horse

6551 Telegraph Ave at 66th ☎510/652-3820, ⓦwww .whitehorsebar.com. Oakland's oldest gay bar – a smallish, friendly place, with mixed dancing for men and women nightly.

Yoshi's World Class Jazz House

in Jack London Square ☎510/238-9200, ⓦwww.yoshis.com. A combination jazz club and sushi bar that routinely attracts the biggest names in jazz. Cover $6–40.

The Wine Country and Marin County

The land north of San Francisco is lush and rural; if you want to escape the city for a short time, this is the direction to head in. Just over the Golden Gate Bridge is the parkland of Marin County, a fine place for a bracing hike and also the closest site to San Francisco for anyone who wants to see the huge old redwoods that once covered the hillsides. But for a weekend of sipping and sunbathing, you have to go farther north, to the grape-blanketed Napa and Sonoma valleys, which support an ambling lifestyle even teetotalers can enjoy. Wine buffs, though, can ricochet between the restaurants and vineyards that stud the rolling countryside; the wineries here produce America's most impressive vintages, and almost every one is open for tastings.

The Marin Headlands

Marin Headlands Information Center, alongside Rodeo Lagoon ☎415/331-1540, ⓦwww.nps.gov/goga/mahe/. Daily 9.30am–4.30pm.

Coming to the undeveloped Marin Headlands, just across the Golden Gate from San Francisco, you'll find some of the most impressive views of the bridge and the city behind – at least if the fog holds off. The rugged landscape makes it a great place for an isolated clifftop scramble, especially among the ruins of old forts and gun emplacements that date from as recently as World War II back to the Civil War. The park's best-designed hike is the Coastal Trail – also the best biking route – which begins at the northern

▼ DRIVING ACROSS THE GOLDEN GATE BRIDGE

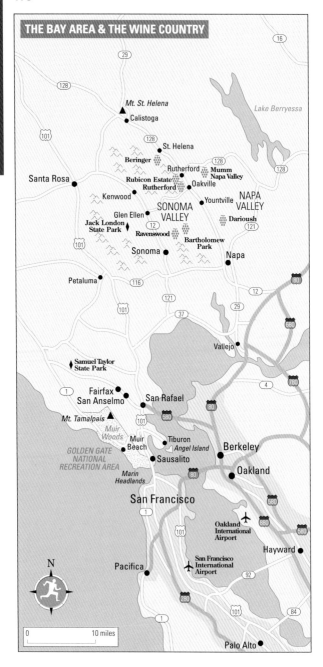

THE BAY AREA & THE WINE COUNTRY

end of Golden Gate Bridge and climbs the mountain facing back toward the city before plunging into Rodeo Valley to the west then looping back.

Muir Woods

☎415/388-2595, ⓦ www.nps.gov/ muwo. Daily 8am–sunset, $3. This forest is home to 556 acres of redwood trees, most of which are more than 500 years old, and which once covered the whole area. Though Muir is a majestic and tranquil spot, where the sunlight filters three hundred feet down from the treetops to the laurel- and fern-covered canyon below, it's also a prime tour destination and is often clogged with busloads of tourists on weekends, so plan a weekday visit if you can.

Napa Valley

As soon as you arrive in Wine Country, it's easy to see why Napa and Sonoma valleys have been so romanticized, with their cool, oak tree–shaded ravines, mineral springs, and chaparral-

covered ridges – more like the rustic Mediterranean than dust-bowl interior California.

The town of Napa itself is an expensive and unremarkable place, noteworthy mostly for its swanky eateries; you're better heading past it to the spring town of Calistoga, which produces the namesake mineral water as well as hosting several curative spas. Sam Brannan, a Gold Rush–era millionaire from San Francisco, first established a resort here in 1860; the (likely apocryphal) story is that the tongue-tied Brannan attempted to dub the town the "Saratoga of California" but mangled the name, with Calistoga the result.

Yountville and Oakville are, these days, little more than yuppie getaways home to upscale restaurants (most famously the ultra-pricey French Laundry – see below) and high-end antiques stores. **St Helena**'s a standout, thanks largely to its impressive architectural haul: Main Street is lined with some of the Wine Country's finest nineteenth-century buildings, while Oak Avenue's crammed with a well-preserved selection of Craftsman-style homes.

Dr Wilkinson's Hot Springs

1507 Lincoln Ave, Calistoga ☎707/942-4102, ⓦ www.drwilkinson .com. Treatments start at $75. The best known of Napa Valley's hot springs hideouts is a health spa–cum–hotel (rates from $109) where you can enjoy heated mineral water treatments or volcanic-ash tension-relieving massages.

Sonoma Valley

Smaller, more rustic, and more welcoming, crescent-shaped Sonoma Valley is home to fewer

▼ MUIR WOODS

PLACES

The Wine Country and Marin County

Information resources

If you want to plan an overnight trip (or longer) to the Wine Country, there's ample information available from the twin local CVBs: Napa Valley Visitors Bureau, 1310 Napa Town Center, downtown Napa (☎707/226-7459, ⓦ www.napavalley.com, daily 9am–5pm) and Sonoma Valley Visitors Bureau, 453 First St East, downtown Sonoma (☎707/996-1090, ⓦ www.sonomavalley.com; daily 9am–5pm, open until 6pm through summer)

wineries than Napa but is also less choked with day-trippers; there are ambling backroads quilting the countryside here, and at least a fleeting sense of laid-back local life. If you have only one day to spend in the Wine Country, scoot past better-known Napa and head here instead; the wineries are slightly less corporate and give a sense of what the vineyards must have been like in the early days – indeed, vine-planting here predates Napa's by more than 20 years.

Many of the local tourist attractions capitalize relentlessly

▼ NAPA VALLEY

not just on the wine made here, but on the area's nickname, Valley of the Moon. It was coined by local Native Americans since the moon seems to rise repeatedly from behind different peaks as you hike through the land here; local boy Jack London retold the story, and it's been associated with Sonoma ever since.

Of the towns here, it's worth stopping in Sonoma itself, filled with dozens of historic Mexican-era buildings, all dotted around a grassy downtown square (in summer, hit it on Tuesday evenings when there's a farmers' market and lively fair from 5 to 9pm). Historically, Sonoma's best known as the site of the Bear Flag Revolt in 1846, which propelled California into independence from Mexico and then into statehood. In the revolt, a few dozen angry Anglo settlers declared their independence here by hoisting a pennant with a bear on it that's the basis for the current state flag. Three weeks later, the United States declared war on Mexico and annexed California without firing a shot.

Jack London State Park

☎707/938-5216, ⓦ www.parks.ca.gov. Daily 9am–5pm, $6 per vehicle. Zip up London Ranch Road past the Beringer winery to find this 140-acre park, land once owned by and now dedicated to the *Call of the Wild* author.

The oddest sight is the ruined Wolf House, a short walk along a trail from the parking lot; the Mayan temple–like frame's all that's left of the mansion that London intended as his future family seat – a 1913 fire burnt it to the ground a month before he could move in. To brush up your London history, hit London Cottage (Sat & Sun, 10am–4pm, free) for a heavily promotional but endearing video recap of his life, his wife Charmian, and his era. It's a refreshingly rural and untouristy part of the Wine Country, and makes a pleasant place to linger on the grass for a sunny afternoon.

Shops

Anette's Chocolate Factory

1321 1st St, Napa ☎707/252-4228, ⓦ www.anettes.com. Artisanal chocolatier that produces quirky, tasty candies all flavored with an extra kick thanks to a slug or two of wine – try the chocolate wine sauce or the Chardonnay-infused caramel brittle.

Enoteca Wine Shop

1348b Lincoln Ave, Calistoga ☎707/942-1117, ⓦ www .enotecawineshop.com. If you don't find what you want at one of the wineries themselves, hit this local-favorite wine shop, which stocks both hard-to-find vintages and new blends.

Wineries

Oddly, despite its fame and the fact that vines have been tended here since missionary days, the Napa region doesn't produce much wine (only 4 percent of California's total output); but what it does churn out is far and away the best in the country. The industry here was kick-started when German refugee Jacob Beringer recognized that the rocky, well-drained soil around here duplicated that of his wine-producing homeland; in 1875, he started producing California vintages, and his namesake winery is the oldest continually operating in the country.

These days, Beringer's bolt-hole is just one of almost 400 wineries sprawled across the valleys, all of which are comfortably geared to handle hordes of visitors. Recently, some wineries in Napa – in an attempt to whittle down their visitors to true buffs – have hiked prices and required reservations to visit, much like fancy restaurants. It's well worth it, as the experience is more rarefied and less like a freebie free-for-all. We've listed a couple of these such wineries below, along with some cheaper, long-term favorites.

Bartholomew Park Winery

1000 Vineyard Lane, Sonoma ☎707/935-9511, ⓦ www.bartholom-ewparkwinery.com. Self-guided tours of winery and tastings, daily 11am–4.30pm. Tours free, tasting $5. Bartholomew is housed in an enormous Spanish Colonial building and offers a museum of local history where there's an introduction to the rudimentary rules of winemaking. The real lure, though, is its affordable, drinkable wines – it's the best place to pick up a case or two to take home.

Darioush

4240 Silverado Trail, northeast of Napa ☎707/257-2345, ⓦ www.darioush .com. Tastings daily 10.30am–5pm, $15 for four wines, $35 for private tasting with cheese pairings. Owned by an L.A.-based grocery store magnate and modeled on an Iranian palace (the stone was imported from Persia), this winery turns out impressive cabernet sauvignon and Shiraz; it was also one of the first to introduce higher-priced, more exclusive tastings.

Beringer

2000 Main St, St Helena ☎707/963-7115, ⓦwww.beringer.com. Tasting tours daily 10.45am, 1.30pm & 2pm, $10; longer tours, $15–30. Beringer is home to the most famous piece of architecture in the area. The Rhine House was

▼ BERINGER

designed not in the prevailing Mission style but rather in the neo-Gothic tradition, modeled after the Beringer family estate back in Germany. Its wines are uniformly impressive, though the small selection of dessert vintages are standouts.

Mumm Napa Valley

8445 Silverado Trail, Rutherford ☎707/942-3434, ⓦwww .mummnapavalley.com. Free tours daily on the hour 10am–3pm, tastings daily 10am–5pm, $5–12. Co-owned by the French Champagne house, the Mumm winery produces fizzy and fresh sparkling wines – but it's also famous for its chatty,

high-energy tours that avoid too much hard selling.

Ravenswood

18701 Gehricke Rd, Sonoma
☎707/933-2332, ⓦwww.ravenswood-wine.com. Tours daily by reservation only at 10.30am, tasting room open 10am–4.30pm. $5. For pure unpretentious fun your best bet is Ravenswood, which lives up to its scrappy slogan, "No Wimpy Wines," by producing robust zinfandels and even hosting friendly barbecues in its tasting rooms during the summer.

Rubicon Estate

1991 St Helena Highway, Rutherford
☎707/968-1100 or 1-800/782-4266, ⓦwww.rubiconestate.com. Tours daily by reservation 10am–5pm. Formerly Niebaum-Coppola, this Inglenook estate is one of the new, high-charging spots. For $25 a person, you'll get five tastings, including a sample of the signature $110-per-bottle Rubicon Estate wine, as well as the chance to ogle two floors of movie memorabilia in the chateau (including Coppola's Oscars).

Cafés

Café Sarafornia

1413 Lincoln Ave, Calistoga
☎707/942-0555. This down-home diner is famous for its cheap, delicious breakfasts and lunches, not to mention its chatty owner. Expect a wait at the weekend.

The Coffee Garden

421 1st St W, Sonoma ☎707/996-6645. Fresh sandwiches are served on the back patio of this 150-year-old adobe café; there's a small (if unremarkable) gift shop on site, too.

Restaurants

Bouchon

6534 Washington St, Yountville
☎707/944-8037, ⓦwww.bouchonbistro.com. Thomas Keller "casual" alternative to the French Laundry is still an haute cuisine temple to Cal cooking, though the menu here's more French-influenced (think lashings of foie gras). Entrées run around $30.

French Laundry

6640 Washington St, Yountville
☎707/944-2380, ⓦwww.frenchlaundry.com. Housed in a small stone building, this famed gourmet hotspot, arguably the best restaurant on the West Coast, serves outstanding Californian cuisine – you'll need to dress up (jackets, no jeans) and reserve a table two months in advance (call first thing in the morning, too). True foodies can gorge on the chef's tasting menu ($210 per person, without wine), which sprawls over nine courses and usually features classics of French cuisine like foie gras and crème brûlée.

Greystone Restaurant at the Culinary Institute of America

2555 Main St, St. Helena
☎707/967-1010, ⓦwww.ciachef.edu/restaurants/wsg. This elegant, ivy-walled mansion with a trippy Art Deco interior by Adam Tihany is handily set just outside town and offers visitors the chance to sample Cal-French specialties like pan-roasted magret of duck ($29) and noisettes of clover-fed veal loin ($30).

La Casa

121 E Spain St, Sonoma ☎707/996-3406. Friendly, festive, and inexpensive Mexican restaurant

just across from the Sonoma Mission – the enchiladas are especially tasty.

Press

587 St. Helena Highway, St. Helena ☎707/967-0550, ⓦwww.presssthelena .com. Everyone's talking about this sceney new spot in a rustic farmhouse setting that serves wood oven–charred meats like baby leg of lamb and wild fish; its high profile is thanks to owner Leslie Rudd, who's also a partner at famed grocery Dean & Deluca. Budget $60 a head plus wine.

Stomp

1457 Lincoln Ave, Calistoga ☎707/942-8272 ⓦwww .stomprestaurant.com. Café-restaurant with a casual bar where you can order snacks from the main menu and a dressier eatery serving sumptuous but simple dishes

like creamy cauliflower soup or trio of roasted beets ($8–12) as well as mains including basil-crusted lamb chop and seared sea bass ($24–30).

Bars

Amigos Grill & Cantina

19315 Sonoma Highway, Sonoma ☎707/939-0743. If you've had your fill of vintage Chardonnays, cap the day with a stop here for a margarita or two, blended from your choice of almost two dozen tequilas.

Downtown Joe's

902 Main St at 2nd, Napa ☎707/258-2337, ⓦwww.downtownjoes.com. Lively, no-nonsense sports bar with an outdoor terrace and on-site brewery that's still hopping with locals come midnight. evenings.

Accommodation

Hotels

Hotels in San Francisco are plentiful, and there's a wide variety to choose from, but don't expect too many bargains: rooms will usually cost at least $110 per night. There's the usual raft of big-name hotels; but if you're looking for local charm, there's a cluster of boutique hotel groups, including Kimpton (wwww .kimptongroup.com), Joie de Vivre (wwww.jdvhospitality .com), and Personality (wwww .personalityhotels.com), that are a quirkier option – we've included our pick of their properties in the selections below. As for location, the densest concentration of rooms can be found around Union Square (including Chinatown and the Theater District) – this is a handy place to stay for public transit, and since there are so many rooms, you should be able to haggle during off-season since the cheaper hotels are gasping for business. If you're driving, it's easier and cheaper to stay further out, especially since parking, nightmarishly expensive downtown, is often included in the overnight rate at motels on the waterfront or in the city's western districts.

Union Square and the Theater District

Allison Hotel/Amber Court 417 Stockton St at Sutter ☎415/956-8200 wwww .harsch.com/bay_area/hotel/TheAllison Hotel.htm. The Allison will be renamed the Amber Court early in 2007 after several years of renovation. It has the floral bedspreads standard for budget hotels, but nifty touches like flatscreen TVs elevate it above the ordinary, as do the gleaming new white bathrooms. The rooms with views over the air well are dark, so ask for one overlooking the street.

Campton Place 340 Stockton St at Sutter, ☎415/781-5555 or 1-800/235-4300, wwww.camptonplace.com. Upscale and understated hotel that provides utter seclusion, as well as terrific views, despite being located in the heart of Union Square. Just purchased by boutique firm KOR, expect the Deco-inspired rooms to undergo a swanky makeover soon. $340

Clift 495 Geary St at Taylor ☎415/775-4700 or 1-800/652-5438, wwww .clifthotel.com. The rooms at this Ian Schrager outpost are vaguely Asian and vintage Starck, with quirky touches like mirrored Louis XIV–style chairs. It's pricey, swish, and ultra-cool; just don't expect smiles from the staff. Note that the walls here are very thin, so bring earplugs. Rates start at $220.

Accommodation practicalities

The Visitor Information Center (see Essentials, p.197) can provide the latest accommodation options, while San Francisco Reservations (Mon–Fri 6am–11pm, Sat–Sun 8am–11pm; ☎1-800/677-1500, wwww.hotelres.com) will find you a room from around $120 a double. British visitors can reserve rooms through Colby International (Mon–Fri 10am–5pm GMT; ☎0151/220 5848, wwww.colbyintl.com).

For B&Bs, contact a specialist agency such as Bed and Breakfast San Francisco (Mon–Fri 9am–5.30pm, ☎415/899-0060 ☎ 415/899-9923, wwww.bbsf.com).

Rates in this chapter refer to the approximate cost of a double room throughout most of the year; be aware that rates rise, sometimes significantly, at peak times and that for hotels, motels, and bed and breakfasts you will have to pay room tax – currently 14 percent of the total bill – on top of these rates.

ACCOMMODATION

ACCOMMODATION

Adagio	25
Adelaide Hostel	23
Allison Hotel/Baldwin	17
Amber Court	19
Argonaut	2
Best Western Carriage Inn	38
Best Western Tuscan Inn	3
Boheme	5
Campton Place	21
Clift Hotel	29
Commodore International	20
Fairmont	10
Grant	14
Green Tortoise Hostel	7
HI-Downtown	30
HI-Fisherman's Wharf	1
Hotel des Arts	16
Hotel Diva	26
Hotel Vitale	31
Huntington	11
Inter-Continental Mark Hopkins	12
Monaco	28
Mosser	35
Orchard Hotel	15
Pacific Tradewinds Guesthouse	9
Palace Hotel	27
Palomar	34
Phoenix	33
Prescott	22
Renoir	37
Royal Pacific Motor Inn	8
San Remo	4
St Regis	32
SW Hotel	6
Triton	18
Westin St Francis	24
White Swan Inn	13
YMCA	36

Commodore Hotel 825 Sutter St at Jones, ☎415/923-6800 or 1-800/338-6848, ⓦ www.thecommodorehotel.com. Rooms here are decorated in warm, earthy colors, offset by shiny steel neo-Deco fixtures; the refurbished bathrooms are blindingly white and clean. Though the decorations don't vary, each room is named after a local attraction like the Haas Lilienthal House or the Mission murals. The great *Canteen* restaurant (see p.73) is a plus. Rooms from $99.

Hotel Adagio 550 Geary St at Jones ☎415/775-5000 or 1-800/228-8830, ⓦ www.thehoteladagio.com. The decor at this hotel echoes its ornate Spanish Revival facade with deep reds and ochres, and the large rooms are well appointed with all mod cons. The Adagio also provides free use of computers with high-speed Internet access and even free printing facilities. Rooms start at $165.

Hotel des Arts 447 Bush St at Grant, ☎415/956-3232 or 1-800/956-4322, ⓦ www.sfhoteldesarts.com. Hybrid art gallery and hotel: half of the rooms here are custom-decorated by local artists and there are pictures for sale all over the lobby's stark white walls. Most of the rooms are en suite, although a few of the undecorated ones are cheaper, with "European-style" baths in the hallway. From $69 for an undecorated room with shared bath; $110 for an artist-decorated room with private bath.

Hotel Diva 440 Geary St at Taylor ☎415/885-0200 or 1-800/553-1900, ⓦ www.hoteldiva.com. The sleek, steel lobby at this boutique hotel echoes the rooms, which are large and minimalist, with brushed metal furniture and huge, comfy beds. Rooms are $169 and up.

Monaco 501 Geary St at Taylor ☎415/292-0100 or 1-800/214-4220, ⓦ www.monaco-sf.com. A quirky boutique hotel housed in a historic Beaux Arts building that features canopied beds in each highly colored, rather overwrought room. It's known for providing complimentary goldfish to keep lonely travelers company at night. Rooms from $189.

Orchard Hotel 665 Bush St at Powell ☎415/362-8878, ⓦ www.theorchardhotel.com. Upscale boutique hotel with great staff, stylish decor (like a Regency-era gentlemen's club), and state-of-the-art entertainment gadgets in most rooms. $149 and up.

Prescott 545 Post St at Mason ☎415/563-0303 or 1-800/283-7322, ⓦ www.prescotthotel.com. Opulent hotel with large rooms decorated in warm woods and rich colors. Service is flawless – attentive and polite – and the amenities offered with concierge-level rooms, like free breakfast and evening drinks, make the splurge worthwhile. Rates from $199.

Westin St Francis 335 Powell St at Sutter ☎415/397-7000 or 1-800/WESTIN1, ⓦ www.westinstfrancis.com. This landmark's sumptuous lobby features a great grandfather clock (the *Westin*'s unofficial mascot), an ornate ceiling, and a gauche painting of Queen Elizabeth. It's been the site of many scandals over the years – including the attempted assassination of Gerald Ford – but frankly, the rooms are disappointingly plain after such a riotous entrance. They start at $149.

Chinatown

Baldwin Hotel 321 Grant Ave at Bush ☎415/781-2220 or 1-800/622-5394, ⓦ www.baldwinhotel.com. Surprisingly quiet, given this hotel's hub location in the heart of Chinatown, with simply furnished, neutral-colored rooms. Rates are negotiable off-season and generally begin at $89.

Grant Hotel 753 Bush St at Mason ☎415/421-7540 or 1-800/522-0979, ⓦ www.granthotel.net. A good value considering its central location, this hotel has small but clean rooms, over-powered a little by the relentlessly maroon carpets. Basic but convenient. Rooms from $50.

Hotel Triton 342 Grant Ave at Bush ☎415/394-0500 or 1-888/553-1900, ⓦ www.hoteltriton.com. Trippy, eccentric hotel that offers modern amenities like a 24-hour gym and in-room fax as well as weirder services like nightly Tarot card readings. The rooms themselves are stylish but gaudy and start at $139.

North Beach

Hotel Boheme 444 Columbus Ave at Vallejo ☏415/433-9111, ⓦwww .hotelboheme.com. A smallish hotel with tiny but dramatic rooms featuring canopied beds and Art Deco–ish bathrooms decked out in rich, dark colors. Ask for a room at the back if you're a light sleeper. Rates begin at $149.

Royal Pacific Motor Inn 661 Broadway at Columbus ☏415/781-6661 or 1-800/545-5574 ⓦwww.citysearch.com/sfo /royalpacific. This renovated motel is one of the best deals downtown, especially if you're touring California – the room rate includes one free parking space. Rooms here are large, with standard floral bedspreads. There's an onsite gym and sauna, as well as a guest laundry room. Rates from $86.

San Remo Hotel 2237 Mason St at Chestnut ☏415/776-8688 or 1-800/352-7366, ⓦwww.sanremohotel.com. Known for its chatty, helpful staff, this warren-like converted house has cozy, chintzy rooms, all of which share spotless bathrooms. Note that there are no phones or TVs in the bedrooms and no elevator, but the low prices still make it a bargain. Rooms from $50.

SW Hotel 615 Broadway at Grant ☏415/362-2999 or 1-888/595-9188, ⓦwww.swhotel.com. This well-located hotel has rooms decorated in modern Asian style, with carved armoires and headboards, plus bright yellow bedspreads. Rates start at $99.

Nob Hill

Fairmont 950 Mason St at Sacramento ☏415/772-5000 or 1-800/441-1414, ⓦwww.fairmont.com. Most famous of the city's top-notch hotels, this gaudy palace has fantastic views from the rooms, which are luxurious but not thrilling. Don't miss the *Tonga* Room bar (see p.98) in the basement. Rates start at $289.

Huntington Hotel 1075 California St at Taylor ☏415/474-5400, ⓦwww .huntingtonhotel.com. Bogart and Bacall lived for several years at this landmark hotel, which has elegant (in an old-money sort of way) common areas and large if unexciting rooms, many of which have kitchenettes. Rooms from $339.

Inter-Continental Mark Hopkins 1 Nob Hill, 999 California St at Mason ☏415/392-3434 or 1-800/NOB-HILL, ⓦwww.markhopkins.net. A grand, castle-like hotel that was once the chic choice of writers and movie stars but is now more corporate in design and atmosphere. Rooms are decorated in a vaguely Art Deco style, heavy on creams and blacks – though all are identical, prices rise as the floors do. The hotel's also home to the *Top of the Mark* bar (see p.98). Rates start at $355.

Fisherman's Wharf

Argonaut Hotel 495 Jefferson St at Hyde ☏415-397-5572 or 1-866/415-0704, ⓦwww.argonauthotel.com. This brand-new, nautical-themed hotel (there's an anchor motif running through much of the decoration) in the Cannery complex has large, lush rooms that feature DVD players, stereos, and impressive views. Surprisingly quiet for its location. Rooms start at $149.

Best Western Tuscan Inn 425 North Point at Mason ☏415/561-1100 or 1-800/648-4626, ⓦwww.tuscaninn.com. Despite its name, this waterfront hotel is more English country manor than Tuscan farmhouse, with cozy rooms decorated in warm colors. It has attentive touches like an afternoon wine reception and a free limo to downtown in the mornings. Rooms $159 and up.

Pacific Heights and Cow Hollow

Hotel Del Sol 3100 Webster St at Lombard ☏415/921-5520 or 1-877/433-5765, ⓦwww.thehoteldelsol.com. The best place for budget cool in the city, this funky, mosaic-wrapped motor lodge has a tropical theme, as well as a swimming pool, all done out in zesty colors; ditto the basic but bright rooms. Rooms are $95 and up.

Hotel Drisco 2901 Pacific Ave at Broderick ☏415/346-2880 or 1-800/634-7277, ⓦwww.hoteldrisco.com. A super-luxurious hotel at the peak of Pacific Heights with spectacular city views and attentive, unobtrusive service. Overall it feels more like a country B&B than a hotel, thanks to the parlor-like common areas. There are VCRs in every room and complimentary sherry every afternoon. Rooms from $195.

Queen Anne 1590 Sutter St at Octavia ☎415/441-2828 or 1-800/227-3970, ⓦwww.queenanne.com. Gloriously overdone restored Victorian (it began as a girls' school before becoming a bordello) where each room is stuffed with gold-accented Rococo furniture and bunches of silk flowers. The late Miss Mary Lake, former principal of the school, is said to still make periodic supernatural appearances in room 410. Rooms from $99.

Surf Motel 2265 Lombard St at Pierce ☎415/922-1950. This old-school motel has two tiers of bright, simple rooms that are sparklingly clean. Be sure to ask for a room at the back to escape the noise from the street. Rates start at $60.

SoMa

Best Western Carriage Inn 140 7th St at Mission ☎415/552-8600 or 1-800/444-5817, ⓦwww.carriageinnsf.com. The enormous, elegant rooms with sofas and working fireplaces, plus free breakfast, come close to making up for the location on a slightly sketchy block. Rates begin at $129.

Hotel Palomar 12 4th St at Market ☎415/348-1111 or 1-877/294-9711, ⓦwww.hotelpalomar.com. Chic, neo-Nouveau bolt-hole, with a dark and smoky color scheme, plus ebony and leopard-print accents; the rooms are pleasantly large and packed with amenities including fax machines. Rooms from $199.

Hotel Vitale 8 Mission St at the Embarcadero ☎415/278-3700, ⓦwww .hotelvitale.com. New, vaguely spa-themed upscale hotel has enormous, art-filled rooms, with comfy beds, flatscreen TVs, and sofas in the window bays so you can make the most of the spectacular setting by the bay. Bizarrely, former mayor Willie Brown broadcasts his morning radio show every day from the bar here. $230 and up.

The Mosser 54 4th St at Market ☎415/986-4400, ⓦwww.themosser .com. A cool recent conversion that fuses Victorian touches like ornamental molding with mod leather sofas. Though the chocolate- and olive-colored rooms are tiny, each is artfully crammed with amenities, including multi-disc CD players. Rooms from $109.

Palace 2 New Montgomery St at Market ☎415/512-1111, ⓦwww.sfpalace.com. Hushed, opulent building, well known for its famous Garden Court tearoom (a favorite of presidents and heads of state); though you'll enjoy the cachet of staying here, the gold and green English country house–style rooms are small for the sky-high prices. Rates $550 and up.

St Regis 125 Third St at Mission ☎415/284-4000, ⓦwww.stregis.com/ sanfrancisco. With spectacular views over SFMOMA, this high-rise ultra-luxe spot has killer, five-star rooms with vaguely Asian wooden screens on the walls and Brancusi-inspired sculptures. There are enormous tubs for deep soaking, huge beds, and touchscreen controls in the bedside drawer to dim lighting or summon room service. $560 and up.

Tenderloin and Civic Center

Phoenix Hotel 601 Eddy St at Larkin ☎415/776-1380 or 1-800/248-9466, ⓦwww.thephoenixhotel.com. This raucous, retro motel conversion is a favorite with up-and-coming bands when they're in town. There's a small pool, and the 44 rooms are eclectically decorated in tropical colors with changing local artwork on the walls. Rates start at $109.

Renoir Hotel 45 McAllister St at 7th ☎415/626-5200 or 1-800/576-3388, ⓦwww.renoirhotel.com. This hotel's location in a wedge-shaped building overlooking Market Street makes it especially popular during Gay Pride for the views along the parade route. The rooms (from $89) have recently been florally, if unexcitingly, refurbished.

The Castro

Beck's Motor Lodge 2222 Market St at Sanchez ☎415/621-8212 or 1-800/227-4360. The clientele here is more mixed than you'd expect from its Castro location, and the soft, bluish rooms are plusher than the gaudy yellow motel exterior might suggest. Rates start at $100.

Haight-Ashbury and around

Hayes Valley Inn 417 Gough St at Hayes ☎415/431-9131 or 1-800/930-7999, ⓦwww.hayesvalleyinn.com. This secluded inn has homey, apple-green rooms with a well-stocked kitchen/breakfast nook that's a great place to meet people (a hefty continental breakfast is included in the room rate). Note that bathrooms are all shared. Rooms from $78.

Stanyan Park 750 Stanyan St at Waller ☎415/751-1000, ⓦwww.stanyanpark.com. A small, neat hotel overlooking Golden Gate Park – its sumptuous, heavily draped rooms with four posters are oddly incongruous in its countercultural neighborhood. $130 and up.

The Richmond and the Sunset

Ocean Park Motel 2690 46th Ave at Wawona ☎415/566-7020, ⓦwww.oceanparkmotel.citysearch.com. San Francisco's first Art Deco motel is an outstanding example of Streamline Moderne architecture. It's also convenient to the beach and the zoo, plus there's a kids' play area. Rooms from $65.

Oceanview Motel 4340 Judah St at LaPlaya ☎415/661-2300, ⓦwww.oceanviewmotel.citysearch.com. No-frills lodging out in the Sunset District, with smallish, simply furnished rooms. There's free on-site parking and convenient Muni access. Rates start at $65.

Bed and breakfasts

San Francisco is filled with fancy B&Bs, most of them housed in historic buildings – in fact, staying at a B&B is an easy way to see the interior of a fully-restored Victorian up close. And if you're set on staying in Haight-Ashbury or the Castro, B&Bs are really the only choice, since large hotels have yet to invade those areas. Be aware, though, that you'll often be opting for the charms of a home-cooked breakfast in exchange for sharing a shower. Expect rates to start around $100, higher in summer; all will usually include a hearty breakfast and afternoon tea and sherry; we've noted, where applicable, the premium some charge for a private bathroom.

24 Henry 24 Henry St at Sanchez, Castro ☎415/864-5686 or 1-800/900-5686, ⓦwww.24henry.com. Tucked away on a leafy residential street, this small B&B is a predominantly gay male guesthouse with five simple rooms, only one with private bath. $75 and up.

Archbishop's Mansion 1000 Fulton St at Steiner, Alamo Square ☎415/563-7872 or 1-800/543-5820, ⓦwww.jdvhospitality.com/hotels/hotel/2. The last word in camp elegance, this B&B hotel stands on the corner of Alamo Square and is crammed with $1 million worth of antiques, including the chandelier from *Gone with the Wind*. Each of the grand rooms is named after a different Italian opera – the largest (and priciest) is Don Giovanni. Rooms begin at $289.

The Carl 198 Carl St at Stanyan, Haight-Ashbury ☎415/661-5679 or 1-888/661-5679, ⓦwww.citysearch.com/sfo/carl-hotel. A plain B&B that's a bargain for its Golden Gate Park location; it has small but pretty floral-decorated rooms that have microwaves and fridges; the six with shared baths are especially well priced. From $75 (private) or $59 (shared).

Inn on Castro 321 Castro St at Market, Castro ☎415/861-0321, ⊛innoncastro .com. Luxurious B&B that's spread across two nearby houses, with eight rooms and three apartments available, all of which are brightly decorated in individual styles and have private phones, high-speed Internet, and DVD players. Shared bath from $115, private bath from $135.

Inn San Francisco 943 South Van Ness Ave at 20th, Mission ☎415/641-0188 ⊛www.innsf.com. Superb, sprawling B&B in two adjoining historic Victorians on the Mission's edge. The 1872 mansion is filled with fresh flowers and has wi-fi throughout; its fifteen rooms are dark and stylish. The 1904 extension next door holds six more rooms, which are chintzier in décor with frilly valances and tapestries. Private bath from $125, shared bath from $95.

Red Victorian Bed, Breakfast and Art 1665 Haight St at Cole, Haight-Ashbury ☎415/864-1978, ⊛www.redvic.com. Bizarre B&B and "Peace Center," decorated with the owner's ethnic arts, where rooms vary from simple to opulent. Breakfast's a lavish but concertedly communal affair, so be prepared to chat with your neighbors while you eat. Most rooms share common baths. Shared bath rates start at $86, private bath from $120.

White Swan Inn 845 Bush St at Mason, Union Square ☎415/775-1755 or 1-800/999-9570, ⊛www.jdvhospitality .com/hotels/hotel/16 Top-tier B&B with a serious English manor theme, what with all the roaring fireplaces, oak-paneled rooms, and afternoon tea. Rooms from $180.

Hostels

San Francisco's hostels are first-rate and an exceptionally good value for the amenities on offer – from free Internet terminals to curfew-free, 24-hour access. All the ones we've listed below are spotless and friendly, with a liberal, laid-back vibe and a welcoming staff. At most hostels, whether privately run or part of the HI (Hosteling International) network, a dorm bed will cost around $20–25, but since space is tight downtown and all these places are wildly popular, make sure to book ahead in high season. In each account, we've noted the specific amenities that are included in the price.

Adelaide Hostel 51 Isadora Duncan Lane off Taylor Street at Geary, Theater District ☎415/359-1915 or 1-877/359-1915, ⊛www.adelaidehostel.com. Hidden away on a tiny lane close to Union Square, this hostel features 100 beds spread across 4-, 6-, and 10-person dorms; some have en suite bathrooms, others share bathrooms nearby. The unbeatable facilities include a big, peaceful, sofa-filled lounge, free wi-fi, and a backyard deck. 24 hours. Highly recommended. Dorms $20 per person, private rooms from $55.

Elements Hostel 2524 Mission St at 21st, Mission t415/647-4100 or 1-866/327-8407, ⊛www.elementssf .com. Mission Street newbie with en-suite dorm rooms (single sex and mixed) Amenities include 24-hour access, wi-fi and Internet access, movie showings, a hearty continental breakfast, linens, and towels. Dorms $25 per person, private rooms $30 per person. Rates rise 20 percent in July and August.

Green Tortoise 494 Broadway at Montgomery, North Beach ☎415/834-1000 or 1-800/867-8647, ⊛www.greentortoise .com. Laid-back hostel with dorm beds and double rooms (with shared bath). Extras include free Internet access, use of the small on-site sauna, and complimentary breakfast; there's no curfew. $23–25 dorm beds, private rooms $56–65.

HI–San Francisco **Fisherman's Wharf Building 240, Fort Mason** ☏415/771-7277, ⓦwww.norcalhostels.org. This is a choice budget option for an outdoorsy traveler, a standard hostel on the waterfront in a park close to Fisherman's Wharf and housed in a historic Civil War–era barracks. It doesn't require a membership fee, so it's even cheaper than hostels elsewhere; dorm beds cost $22.

HI–San Francisco Downtown **312 Mason St at Geary** ☏415/788-5604, ⓦwww.norcalhostels.org. This hostel's four-person dorms are spotless, with bathroom facilities shared by eight people, while private rooms are pricier and sleep two; it's open 24 hours, and there's a kitchen with microwave. Reservations recommended. $23 members, $26 nonmembers; private rooms $67 mems, $70 nonmems.

Pacific Tradewinds Guesthouse **680 Sacramento St at Kearny, Chinatown** ☏415/433-7970 or 1-800/486-7975, ⓦwww.san-francisco-hostel.com. The best budget option in the center of town, this small hostel offers free high-speed Internet access and a clean kitchen, plus a large, communal dining table that's an easy way to get to know fellow travelers. Dorms are $24 per person.

YMCA Central Branch **220 Golden Gate Ave at Leavenworth** ☏415/885-0460, ⓦwww.centralymcasf.org. Simple rooms, but a great deal nonetheless – $12 overnight parking, free breakfast, and free use of YMCA fitness center. There are private rooms with bath as well as a few dorms. $23.50 dorm bed, $73.56 room with private bath (prices include tax).

Essentials

Arrival

Unless you're coming from nearby on the West Coast, the quickest way to get to San Francisco is by flying. There are also plenty of routes in by bus; Amtrak trains run to neighboring Oakland.

By air

All international and most domestic flights arrive at San Francisco International Airport, or SFO (⊕1-800/435-9736 or 650/821-8211, ⓦwww.flysfo.com), located about fifteen miles south of the city.

There are several ways of getting into town from here, each of which is clearly signed from the baggage claim areas. Most people take minibus shuttles into the city – companies include Supershuttle and American Airporter: the vans depart every five minutes from the center island on the road outside the upper level and will take passengers to any city-center destination for around $12 a head; in light traffic, bank on a thirty-minute journey, but allow more time at rush hour. Be ruthless when negotiating prices – competition for these and the several other companies running shuttle services is fierce and lines non-existent. The SFO Airporter bus is slightly cheaper ($10) and makes pickups outside each baggage claim area every fifteen minutes; the snag is that it only serves major hotels downtown. These services are tagged as "Airporter" on the lower arrivals level.

The best option is the BART link: the effortless thirty-minute nonstop train journey whisks you from the airport to the heart of downtown for only $5.15 (ⓦwww.bart.gov) and leaves every 15–20 minutes.

Taxis from the airport cost $25–30 (plus tip) for any downtown location – definitely worth it if you're in a group or too tired to care.

By train and bus

All of San Francisco's Greyhound services currently use the Transbay Terminal at 425 Mission St at 1st, SoMa (⊕1-800/231-2222 or 415/495-1569, ⓦwww.greyhound.com). Plans are afoot to redevelop the terminal, so call to confirm first. To connect from here to the BART network, walk one block north to the Embarcadero station on Market Street.

All Amtrak trains stop in Oakland at Jack London Square (⊕1-800/USA-RAIL or 209/832-8350, ⓦwww.amtrak.com). Free shuttle buses run from the Oakland station across the Bay Bridge to the Transbay Terminal, or you can take BART into town – the Lake Merritt stop is a few blocks' walk northeast of here. A more efficient route is to get off Amtrak at Richmond to the north, where you can easily pick up BART nearby at the Richmond station.

By car

If you're driving into town from the east, the main route is I-80, which runs via Sacramento all the way from Chicago. I-5, fifty miles east of San Francisco, serves as the main north-south route, connecting Los Angeles with Seattle; the I-580 spur from I-5 takes you to the Bay Area. Picking up a car at the airport, head for Hwy-101 North. Stay on this road until you hit the city.

Information

The outstanding San Francisco Visitor Information Center is on the lower level of Hallidie Plaza at the end of the cable car line on Market Street at Powell (Mon–Fri 9am–5pm, Sat–Sun 9am–3pm, ⊕415/283-0177 or recorded information line ⊕415/283-0177,

ⓦwww.sfvisitor.org). There are free maps of the city as well as pamphlets on hotels and restaurants. The center also sells the City Pass ($49; ⓦwww.citypass.net), a half-price ticket valid for entry to several key museums including SFMOMA and either the California Palace of the Legion of Honor or the de Young museum (your choice), passage on a Blue and Gold Fleet San Francisco Bay cruise, plus the best thing of all – a free week's pass on Muni transit.

For information about what's on, try the Sunday edition of the San Francisco Chronicle newspaper ($1.50; ⓦwww .sfgate.com); it includes a section known as the Datebook (also known as the "Pink Pages") that has previews and reviews for the coming week. A new, more family-friendly entertainment supplement, 96 hours, is bundled free with Thursday's paper (50¢). Otherwise, pick up one of the two terrific free weeklies: the Bay Guardian (ⓦwww.sfbg.com) and SF Weekly (ⓦwww.sfweekly.com), available from racks around town, both of which offer more in-depth features on local life and better music and club listings than the Chronicle. As for local magazines, the free monthly PaperCity is a fine source for trendier types; San Francisco magazine ($4.99; ⓦwww.sanfran.com) is the long-established, rather toothless local glossy, while 7x7 is its upstart, slightly more exciting rival ($4; ⓦwww.7x7mag .com). Both are often available free in hotels.

Useful websites

Citysearch ⓦ www.sanfrancisco .citysearch.com. This megasite is a great place to track down a phone number or check a map; be careful, though, as some listings and reviews are out of date.

Craigslist ⓦ www.craigslist.org. The definitive community website started in San Francisco – locals swear by it. A fantastic resource for everything from jobs to concert tickets.

San Francisco Arts ⓦwww.sfarts.org. Comprehensive listings of all things arty – you can search by date and discipline (dance, theater, music) to find exactly what you're looking for.

Mister SF ⓦwww.mistersf.com. Eclectic, opinionated one-man city 'zine that's full of unexpected nuggets of local knowledge.

SF Raves ⓦ www.sfraves.org. Insider guide to nightlife with underground listings for clubs that are edgy and on the mark.

SF Station ⓦ www.sfstation.com. Arguably the best local listings site – opinionated, up-to-date, and easy to use.

City transportation

San Francisco is one of those rare American cities where you don't need a car to see everything: in fact, given the chronic shortage of parking downtown, horrible traffic, and zealous traffic wardens, it makes more sense to avoid driving entirely. The public transportation system covers every neighborhood and is inexpensive to boot. If you have stout legs to tackle those hills, consider cycling – but, frankly, walking the city is still the best bet (though even walkers should note that the steep gradients, especially around Nob Hill, can turn what looks like a five-minute walk on a map into a huffing, puffing, fifteen-minute climb). If you have questions about any form of public transit in the Bay Area, call ☎511 or check ⓦwww.511.org, which even has a point-to-point bus/train route planner.

Muni

Muni (☎415/673-6864, ⓦwww.sfmuni .com) is a comprehensive network of buses, trolley buses, and cable cars. Aside from buses and three picturesque cable car routes, there are five tram lines (see box, opposite) that run underground along Market Street and above ground elsewhere, plus the old-style F tram that shuttles along Market Street, connecting the Embarcadero and the Castro.

On buses and trains the flat fare (correct change only) is $1.50; with each ticket you buy, ask for a free transfer – they're good for another two rides on a train or bus in any direction within ninety minutes to two hours of purchase. Note that cable cars cost $5 one-way and do not accept transfers; a one-day cable car–only pass

Muni tram lines

Muni F–Market Line Restored vintage trolleys from around the world run downtown from the Transbay Terminal up Market Street and into the heart of the Castro. The new extension along the refurbished Embarcadero to Fisherman's Wharf is one of Muni's most popular routes.

Muni J–Church Line From downtown to the Mission and the edge of the Castro.

Muni K–Ingleside Line From downtown through the Castro to Balboa Park.

Muni L–Taraval Line West from downtown through the Sunset to the zoo and Ocean Beach.

Muni M–Ocean View West from downtown by the Stonestown Galleria shopping center and San Francisco State University.

Muni N–Judah Line From the CalTrain station, past AT&T stadium to downtown and west through the Sunset to Ocean Beach.

is $10. A better option – if you don't have a Citypass is an all-Muni Passport pass, available in one-, three-, and seven-day denominations ($11, $18, $24), which is valid for unlimited travel on the Muni system.

BART

Along Market Street downtown, Muni shares station concourses with BART (Bay Area Rapid Transit; ☎510/465-BART or 415/817-1717, ⓦ www.bart.gov), which is the fastest way to get to downtown Oakland and Berkeley, not to mention the Mission District. Tickets aren't cheap ($1.40–5.15, depending on how far you ride), but the service is efficient and dependable; trains follow four routes (which differ mostly only by their East Bay terminus) in a fixed schedule, usually arriving every ten minutes; save your ticket after entering the station as it is also needed when exiting the train. To buy a ticket, insert cash into the automated machine, then use the buttons to reduce the amount by $1 or 5¢ until the appropriate value's reached; then press the print button and pick up both your ticket and change at the same time.

Taxis

Flagging a taxi in San Francisco can be difficult – try hanging around the entrance of one of the larger hotels. Phoning around, try Veterans (☎415/552-1300) or Yellow Cab (☎415/626-2345, ⓦ www.yellocabsf.com). Fares (within the city) begin with a fee of $2.85 to start the meter plus 45¢ for each additional one-fifth of a mile or 60 seconds' waiting time. There's a $2

surcharge to and from SFO airport; expect to add a customary 15 percent tip to the final amount.

Driving

The only reason to rent a car in San Francisco is if you want to explore the larger Bay Area or Wine Country, or drive north or south along the coast (for car rental info, see p.203). If you have to drive in town, pay attention to San Francisco's attempts to control downtown traffic: the posted speed limit is 30mph and pedestrians waiting in a crosswalk always have the right-of-way. In addition, it's almost impossible to make a left turn anywhere downtown, meaning you'll have to get used to looping the block, making three rights instead of one left. Another challenge is parking – there's barely any on-street space, but you'll find plenty of garages – expect to pay $2.50 per fifteen minutes. If you do find a curbside space, note if the curb is painted with any kaleidoscopically colored stripes, especially green (ten-minute limit for all vehicles) or any one of the following three combinations, which mean that private vehicles should not stop at any time: yellow, yellow/black, or yellow/green/black. Also make sure to observe the San Francisco law of curbing wheels on steep streets – turn wheels into the curb if the car points downhill and away from the curb if it points up.

Cycling

Cycling is a fantastic way to experience San Francisco. Golden Gate Park, the Marina and Presidio, and Ocean beach all have great paved trails and some off-road routes. Throughout the city, marked bike routes – with lanes – direct riders to all major points of interest, but note that officials picked the routes for their lack of car traffic, not for the easiest ride. If you get tired, bikes can be carried on most trains and an increasing number of buses. Blaz-

ing Saddles bike store has several locations (℡415/202-8888, ⓦwww.blazingsaddles.com): the most convenient are 1095 Columbus Ave at Francisco, North Beach, and Piers 41 or 43-1/2 and 465 Jefferson St at the Cannery, Fisherman's Wharf. Rental for bikes is $7/hr, $28/day; tandems $11/hr and $48/day.

City tours

As you'd expect from a city as visitor-friendly as San Francisco, there are plenty of tours available to suit most any interest. Undoubtedly the most impressive (and expensive) option comes from San Francisco Helicopter Tours (℡1-800/400-2404 or 650/635-4500, ⓦwww.sfhelicoptertours.com), which provide a variety of spectacular flights over the Bay Area. Prices start at $130 per passenger for a twenty-minute flight.

There are plenty of walking tours available, but one of the best is City Guides (℡415/557-4266, ⓦwww.sfcityguides.org), a terrific free series sponsored by each neighborhood's public library, which also includes themed walks on topics from the Gold Rush to the Beat Generation. Hobnob Tours ℡650/851-1123, ⓦwww.hobnobtours.com. Lively and scurrilous tours around the Nob Hill homes and haunts of Silver Kings and robber barons. Lead guide Valarie Huff is a fact-packed delight. $30; Mon–Fri, 10am, 1.30pm.

For boat cruises around the bay, check out Blue and Gold Fleet (℡415/773-1188, ⓦwww.blueandgoldfleet.com), which offers chilly 60-minute trips with breathtaking views of the bay, leaving from Piers 39 and 41 at Fisherman's Wharf – though be warned that everything may be shrouded in fog, making the price ($18) less than worth it.

Cruisin' the Castro ℡415/255-1821, ⓦwww.cruisinthecastro.com. Local icon Ms Trevor Hailey has retired, handing off her tour to newbie guide Kathy Amendola. Expect a similar experience, offering as much a history lesson as a sightseeing tour ($45, including lunch) Tues–Sat, 10am.

Victorian Home Walk t415/252-9485, ⓦwww.victorianwalk.com. Leisurely tour through Pacific Heights and Cow Hollow, where you'll learn to tell the difference between a Queen Anne, Italianate, and Stick-Style Vic. $20 per person for a two-hour tour. Meet daily 11am by the clock in the lobby of the *Westin St Francis Hotel.*

Money

With an ATM card (and PIN number) you'll have access to cash from machines all over San Francisco, though as anywhere, you may be charged a fee for using a different bank's ATM network. To find the location of the nearest Bay Area ATM, call Amex ℡1-800/CASH-NOW, Visa Plus ℡1-800/843-7587, or Cirrus/Mastercard ℡1-800/424-7787.

Most banks in San Francisco are open Monday–Friday 9am–3pm, and a few are also open on Saturday 9am–noon. For banking services – particularly currency exchange – outside normal business hours and on weekends, try major hotels: the rate won't be as good, but it's the best option in a tight financial corner.

Phones, mail, and email

Greater San Francisco has a single area code – ☎415, and calls within this code are treated as local, while you'll be charged higher rates for the Wine Country (☎707) or the East Bay (☎510).

International visitors who want to use their mobile phones will need to check with their phone provider whether it will work in the US and what the call charges are; from elsewhere in the US, your phone should operate fine, but you may incur roaming charges. To call home internationally: dial 011 + country code + number, minus the initial 0. Country codes are as follows: Australia (61), Canada (1), New Zealand (64), UK & Northern Ireland (44), and Eire (353). As for mail, international letters will usually take about a week to reach their destination; at time of writing, rates were 84¢ for letters and 75¢ for postcards to Europe or Australia, but the US Postal Service is expected to raise those rates again soon. To find a post office or check up-to-date rates, see ☻www.usps.com or call ☎1-800/275-8777.

If you need to check your email while in town (and didn't bring your laptop), you won't have a hard time doing so – especially as San Francisco's consistently topped polls of Most Wired City in the US. Expect to pay around $7/hr at most Internet cafés. If money's tight, head to the public library, where there's free fifteen-minute access for all – you'll have to sign up in advance, and expect a wait.

Public holidays

January

1: New Year's Day

3rd Monday: Dr Martin Luther King Jr's Birthday

February

3rd Monday: President's Day

May

Last Monday: Memorial Day

July

4: Independence Day

September

1st Monday: Labor Day

October

2nd Monday: Columbus Day

November

11: Veterans' Day

4th Thursday: Thanksgiving Day

December

25: Christmas Day

Festivals and holidays

San Francisco has a huge variety of special festivals, the biggest of which are detailed below. Remember that during some of these events, especially Pride, hotels and hostels will book up quickly so make sure to arrange accommodation well in advance. On the national public holidays listed in the box above, stores, banks, and public and federal offices are liable to be closed all day.

Chinese New Year

End of January or early February, depending on the lunar calendar ☎415/982-3000, ✪www.chineseparade.com. Chinatown's even livelier than usual during this weeklong celebration, which culminates in the Golden Dragon Parade, when hundreds of people march through downtown leading a 75-foot-long dragon.

Cherry Blossom Festival

Late April ☎415/563-2313, ✪www.nccbs .org. For two consecutive weekends, Japantown's concrete plazas host a rowdy celebration of all things Japanese. Highlights include a parade from Civic Center with floats and performers and, best of all, the beauty contest to choose the queen of the festival.

Cinco de Mayo

The weekend nearest to May 5 ☎415/206-0577. Commemorating the Mexican victory at the battle of Puebla, this is a two-day party in the Mission – raucous, booze-filled, and great fun. There's a cluster of stalls in Civic Center Plaza, while the official parade runs down Mission Street between 24th and 14th streets.

Bay to Breakers Footrace

Third Sun in May ☎415/359-2800 ✪www.baytobreakers.com. Kooky, campy, and unique, this event nominally involves a 12km footrace beginning at Howard and Spear streets and ending at the ocean (kickoff at 8am), though it's really just another excuse for San Franciscans to go costume-crazy. Most of the 70,000 runners will be sporting outlandish costumes (or even running naked); an unmissable sight if you're in town.

San Francisco LGBT Pride Celebration Parade

Late June ☎415/864-5733, ✪www. sfpride.org. At one of the bigger and more boisterous Gay Pride events in the world, crowds of up to a half-million pack Market Street for an enormous party-cum-parade, then migrate across to City Hall for a giant block party, with outdoor discos, live bands, and numerous craft and food stands.

Halloween

October 31 ☎415/826-1401. Hundreds strut their stuff in this wild, over-the-top parade: though local powers-that-be have been pushing the procession into Civic Center for logistical reasons, the heart and soul of stuff-strutting is certainly still the Castro.

Directory

American Express 455 Market St at First, Financial District ☎415/536-2600; Mon–Fri 9am–5.30pm, Sat 10am–2pm.
Car Rental Alamo ☎1-800/522-9696, Ⓦwww.alamo.com. Avis ☎1-800/230-4898, Ⓦwww.avis.com.
Budget ☎1-800/527-0700, Ⓦwww.budgetrentacar.com. Thrifty ☎1-800/847-4389, Ⓦwww.thrifty.com.
Cigarettes And Smoking Cigarettes are banned in all public indoor spaces (and generally frowned upon everywhere else) but are still available in virtually any food- or drugstore. While many local pubs turn a blind eye to patrons lighting up, be aware that if you're spotted by a beat cop patrolling the neighborhood, you and the bartender can each be given a $75 fine. Some bars – via a complex legal loophole – have managed to preserve a smoking section for puffing patrons: we've noted them in the text.
Consulates UK, 1 Sansome St, Suite 850 at Market, Financial District (Mon–Fri 8.30am–5pm; ☎415/617-1300, Ⓦwww.britainusa.com/sf)
Ireland, 100 Pine St, 33rd flr at Front, Financial District (Mon–Fri 10am–noon, 2–3.30pm; ☎415/392-4214, Ⓔirishcgsf@earthlink.net)
Australia, 575 Market St, 18th flr at Montgomery, Financial District (Mon–Fri 8.45am–1pm, 2–4.45pm; ☎415/536-1970, Ⓦwww.austemb.org)
Germany, 1960 Jackson St at Gough, Pacific Heights (Mon–Fri 9am–noon; ☎415/775-1061, Ⓦwww.germanyinfo.com)
The nearest New Zealand consulate is in Los Angeles: 2425 Olympic Blvd, Suite 600-E, Santa Monica (Mon-Fri 8.30am-1pm, 1.30–4.30pm, ☎310/566-6555, Ⓦwww.nzcgla.com).
Disabled Access Unsurprisingly, all public buildings in San Francisco, including hotels and restaurants, are required to have wheelchair-accessible bathrooms and entrances, while Muni offers kneeling buses – for full listings, check Ⓦwww.accessnca.com. The only place you could hit trouble is on the steep hills, especially Nob and Telegraph.
Drugstores Walgreens 24hr pharmacies: 498 Castro St at 18th, Castro

☎415/861-6276; 3201 Divisadero St at Lombard, Marina ☎415/931-6415.
Electricity 110V AC.
Emergencies ☎911.
Hospitals San Francisco General Hospital, 1001 Potrero Ave at 23rd, Potrero Hill (☎415/206-8000 or 206-8111 for emergency), has a 24hr emergency walk-in service. Castro-Mission Health Center, 3850 17th St at Prosper, Mission (☎415/487-7500) offers a drop-in medical service that charges on a sliding scale depending on income and offers free contraception and pregnancy testing. California Pacific (formerly Davies) Medical Center, Castro and Duboce, Lower Haight (☎415/565-6060) offers 24hr emergency care and a doctors' referral service.
Opening Hours Most museums will be open six or seven days a week, from at least 10am to 5pm, while stores will close at 6 or 7pm Mon–Sat, and slightly earlier on Sunday. As for restaurants, most will be busiest from 6 to 7.30pm, and many will stop serving dinner after 9.30pm A smattering stay open for hungry night owls – we've noted them in the text.
Passport And Visa Office US Citizenship & Immigration Services, 630 Sansome St at Washington, Jackson Square (customer service by phone Mon–Fri 8am–6pm; ☎1-800/375-5283, Ⓦwww.uscis.gov.
Post Office The main post office is at 101 Hyde St at Fulton, Civic Center (Mon–Fri 8.30am–5.30pm, Sat 10am–2pm; ☎1-800/275-8777). Other branches include Sutter Street Station, 150 Sutter St at Montgomery, Financial District (Mon–Fri 8.30am–5pm), and Rincon Finance Station, 180 Steuart St at Mission, SoMa (Mon–Fri 7am–6pm, Sat 9am–2pm).
Religious Services Grace Cathedral on Nob Hill at 1051 Taylor St has an Episcopalian (Anglican) congregation (☎415/749-6300, Ⓦwww.gracecathedral.org), while Catholics can worship at St Mary's Cathedral, 600 California St at Grant (☎415/288-3800, Ⓦwww.oldsaintmarys.org). The grandest synagogue is Congregation Emanu-El, 2 Lake St at Arguello Blvd, at the eastern edge of the Richmond

Fly Less – Stay Longer!

Rough Guides believes in the good that travel does, but we are deeply aware of the impact of fuel emissions on climate change. We recommend taking fewer trips and staying for longer. If you can avoid travelling by air, please use an alternative, especially for journeys of under 1000km/600miles. And always offset your travel at ⓦ www.roughguides.com/climatechange.

District by the Presidio (☎415/751-2535, ⓦwww.emanuelsf.org).
Tax In the city of San Francisco, sales tax of 8.5 percent is added to virtually everything you buy in a store – except food – but isn't part of the marked price. Hotel tax will add 14 percent onto your bill.

Time Zone The West Coast runs on Pacific Standard Time (PST), always three hours behind the East Coast and eight hours behind the UK.

Chronology

Chronology

Early days ▶ San Francisco and its surrounding area are inhabited by the coastal Miwok tribe, about whom little is known.

1579 ▶ Sir Francis Drake overshoots San Francisco bay while sailing in the *Golden Hinde*, landing instead for repairs close to what's now Point Reyes.

1769 ▶ San Francisco Bay is sighted on foot by a Spanish clergy and soldier contingent – led by Gaspar de Portola.

1775 ▶ Juan Manuel de Ayala becomes the first European to sail into the bay, piloting the *San Carlos.*

1776 ▶ **The Presidio** of San Francisco is established by a 200-strong garrison of Spanish soldiers; at the same time, the group builds the first Mission Dolores on the same site as the current structure.

1780s–1840s ▶ The first civilian settlement emerges at a landing spot between the two military outposts. It's named **Yerba Buena** after the minty herb that grows in abundance on the surrounding hills.

1791 ▶ The second – and current – **Mission Dolores** building is completed.

1846 ▶ The **Mexican–American war** breaks out in Texas, leading US forces to occupy California, which was then part of Mexico. Yerba Buena is quickly commandeered by American forces.

1847 ▶ The settlement is officially renamed San Francisco.

1848 ▶ **Gold** is discovered in the Sierra Nevada foothills, 100 miles from San Francisco, sparking the **Gold Rush**.

1849–1854 ▶ The town morphs into a city overnight as more than 100,000 prospectors arrive hoping to dig a fortune out of California's gold rich land.

1859 ▶ **Silver** – later known as the Comstock Lode – is discovered in western Nevada and a second boom begins. Many of the newer fortune hunters are not Americans from the East, but new immigrants, notably from China.

1860s–70s ▶ Transportation is revolutionized: the railways bring wealth and commerce to western America, and the hill-conquering **cable car** opens up large swathes of San Francisco to new, high-end development, among them Nob Hill.

1875 ▶ The **Palace Hotel** is built by William Ralston. Cutting edge technology includes an intercom system and four hydraulic elevators.

1882 ▶ The **Chinese Exclusion Act** is passed, preventing Chinese immigrants from naturalizing or marrying in America. It's the only law ever aimed at a single racial group, the concrete result of simmering resentment against San Francisco's growing Chinese population.

1904 ▶ A.P. Giannini founds the Bank of Italy in North Beach; it later becomes the **Bank of America**.

1906 ▶ An 8.1 magnitude **earthquake** and resulting fire devastate downtown, destroying almost 500 city blocks and 28,000 buildings. The official death toll is pegged at 500, but is likely many thousands more.

1915 ▶ The **Panama Pacific International Exhibition** is held here on newly reclaimed land (now the Marina). It simultaneously showcases innovations from across the world and San Francisco's successful recovery and rebuilding since 1906.

1920 ▶ **Prohibition** forbids the sale of alcohol. Economic confidence of the 1920s brings the **Jazz Age**, and the Barbary Coast is the site of the city's buzziest nightlife.

1922 ▶ The Mediterranean Revival **Castro Theatre** is built.

1928 ▶ Work begins on the Neo-Gothic **Grace Cathedral**. It will take 36 years to finish.

1929 ▶ Wall Street crashes and America enters the **Great Depression**.

1930s The WPA sponsors several projects in the city, including **Coit Tower** and the **murals** on the Maritime Museum.

1934 ▶ Two longshoremen are killed during protests on '**Bloody Thursday**'; San Francisco is paralyzed for four days as workers citywide call a strike.

1937 ▶ The Golden Gate Bridge is built, another WPA project.

1941 ▶ America enters **World War II**. Many sailors, discharged from the navy under suspicion of **homosexuality**, remain in San Francisco and slowly establish a gay community here.

1950s ▶ The **Beat Generation** emerges, headquartered in North Beach and led by writers like Jack Kerouac and Allen Ginsberg.

1953 ▶ Lawrence Ferlinghetti opens **City Lights bookstore**, which championed Beat writings.

1963 ▶ The government shuts down the island prison **Alcatraz** for budget reasons.

1964 ▶ After decades of neglect, the last three of the eight original **cable car** lines are listed on the National Register of Historic Places.

1965–1970s ▶ The hippie scene of **Haight-Ashbury** appears, powered by LSD and experimental rock like the Grateful Dead and Jefferson Airplane. The hippies participate in widespread **protest demonstrations** against US involvement in Vietnam.

1966 ▶ The **Black Panther** movement is established in Oakland. Stanford drop-out and LSD pioneer **Ken Kesey** hosts a "Trips Festival" in Fisherman's Wharf; flyers are handed out asking "Can you pass the acid test?" A human Be-In is later held in Golden Gate Park.

1967 ▶ The so-called '**Summer of Love**' marks the hippie era's high point.

1969 ▸ A deadly stabbing at the Rolling Stones' concert at Altamont brings the hippie movement to a sharp halt. The Stonewall Riots in New York galvanize the city's nascent gay & lesbian rights movement.

1970s ▸ San Francisco becomes known worldwide as a **gay Mecca** centered on the neighborhood of Eureka Valley, better known as The Castro.

1972 ▸ The first commuter train runs on **BART** (Bay Area Rapid Transit). Architect William Pereira builds the **Transamerica Pyramid** building downtown.

1978 ▸ **Harvey Milk**, the first openly gay man to take public office, is assassinated (along with Mayor George Moscone) by fast food-loving bigot Dan White. White will later unsuccessfully use the notorious 'twinkie defense' at his trial.

1980s ▸ **AIDS** ravages the city's gay population.

1987 ▸ Wall Street crashes; Dow Jones index plunges 500 points in a day.

1989 ▸ A 7.1 magnitude **earthquake** strikes. The waterfront freeway at the Embarcadero is so badly damaged it is torn down.

1995 ▸ The new home for **SFMOMA**, a Mario Botta-designed structure in SoMa, opens.

1996 ▸ Soundbite-loving **Mayor Willie Brown** is elected. The city's prosperity increases thanks to its location near soon-to-be tech hub Silicon Valley.

Late 1990s ▸ The Internet-era **dot com boom** transforms the city like a modern Gold Rush, bringing millions of dollars and thousands of new residents.

2000 ▸ The **dot com bust** causes widespread unemployment and bankruptcies.

2003 ▸ **Arnold Schwarzenegger** becomes governor of California.

2004 ▸ Telegenic **Mayor Gavin Newsom** replaces Brown. One of his first acts is to buck state laws against **gay marriage** and offer same-sex couples licenses at City Hall. The marriages are later declared invalid by the state.

2005 ▸ Herzog and De Meuron's splashy new home for the **de Young Museum** opens in Golden Gate Park.

Get Connected!

"Brilliant! ... the unmatched leader in its field"
Sunday Times, London, reviewing The Rough Guide to the Internet

Rough Guide Computing Titles

Blogging • eBay • iPods, iTunes
& music online • The Internet
Macs & OS X • MySpace
Book of Playlists • PCs & Windows
PlayStation Portable • Website Directory

BROADEN YOUR HORIZONS

"The most accurate maps in the world"

San Jose Mercury News

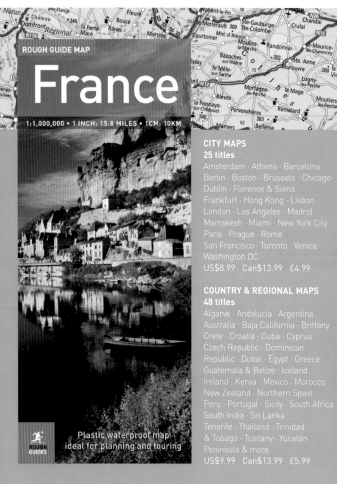

ROUGH GUIDE MAP

France

1:1,000,000 · 1 INCH: 15.8 MILES · 1CM: 10KM

Plastic waterproof map
ideal for planning and touring

CITY MAPS
25 titles
Amsterdam · Athens · Barcelona
Berlin · Boston · Brussels · Chicago
Dublin · Florence & Siena
Frankfurt · Hong Kong · Lisbon
London · Los Angeles · Madrid
Marrakesh · Miami · New York City
Paris · Prague · Rome
San Francisco · Toronto · Venice
Washington DC
US$8.99 Can$13.99 £4.99

COUNTRY & REGIONAL MAPS
48 titles
Algarve · Andalucía · Argentina
Australia · Baja California · Brittany
Crete · Croatia · Cuba · Cyprus
Czech Republic · Dominican
Republic · Dubai · Egypt · Greece
Guatemala & Belize · Iceland
Ireland · Kenya · Mexico · Morocco
New Zealand · Northern Spain
Peru · Portugal · Sicily · South Africa
South India · Sri Lanka
Tenerife · Thailand · Trinidad
& Tobago · Tuscany · Yucatán
Peninsula & more.
US$9.99 Can$13.99 £5.99

waterproof • rip-proof • amazing value

BROADEN YOUR HORIZONS

small print & Index

SMALL PRINT

A Rough Guide to Rough Guides

In 1981, Mark Ellingham, a recent graduate in English from Bristol University, was traveling in Greece on a tiny budget and couldn't find the right guidebook. With a group of friends he wrote his own guide, combining a contemporary, journalistic style with a practical approach to travelers' needs. That first Rough Guide was a student scheme that became a publishing phenomenon. Today, Rough Guides include recommendations from shoestring to luxury and cover hundreds of destinations around the globe, including almost every country in the Americas and Europe, more than half of Africa and most of Asia and Australasia. Millions of readers relish Rough Guides' wit and inquisitiveness as much as their enthusiastic, critical approach and value-for-money ethos. The guides' ever-growing team of authors and photographers is spread all over the world.

In the early 1990s, Rough Guides branched out of travel, with the publication of Rough Guides to World Music, Classical Music and the Internet. All three have become benchmark titles in their fields, spearheading the publication of a range of more than 350 titles under the Rough Guide name, including phrasebooks, waterproof maps, music guides from Opera to Heavy Metal, reference works as diverse as Conspiracy Theories and Shakespeare, and popular culture books from iPods to Poker. Rough Guides also produce a series of more than 120 World Music CDs in partnership with World Music Network.

Visit www.roughguides.com to see our latest publications.

Rough Guide travel images are available for commercial licensing at www.roughguidespictures.com

Publishing information

This second edition published March 2007 by Rough Guides Ltd, 80 Strand, London WC2R 0RL. 345 Hudson St, 4th Floor, New York, NY 10014, USA.

Distributed by the Penguin Group
Penguin Books Ltd, 80 Strand, London WC2R 0RL
Penguin Group (USA), 375 Hudson Street, NY 10014, USA
14 Local Shopping Centre, Panchsheel Park, New Delhi 110017, India
Penguin Group (Australia), 250 Camberwell Road, Camberwell, Victoria 3124, Australia
Penguin Group (Canada), 10 Alcorn Avenue, Toronto, ON M4V 1E4, Canada
Penguin Group (NZ), 67 Apollo Drive, Mairangi Bay, Auckland 1310, New Zealand
Typeset in Bembo and Helvetica to an original design by Henry Iles.

Cover concept by Peter Dyer.

Printed and bound in China
© Rough Guides, March 2007

No part of this book may be reproduced in any form without permission from the publisher except for the quotation of brief passages in reviews.

224pp includes index

A catalogue record for this book is available from the British Library.

ISBN 13: 978-1-84353-751-9

The publishers and authors have done their best to ensure the accuracy and currency of all the information in San Francisco DIRECTIONS, however, they can accept no responsibility for any loss, injury, or inconvenience sustained by any traveler as a result of information or advice contained in the guide.

3   5   7   9   8   6   4   2

Help us update

We've gone to a lot of effort to ensure that the second edition of San Francisco DIRECTIONS is accurate and up-to-date. However, things change – places get "discovered", opening hours are notoriously fickle, restaurants and rooms raise prices or lower standards. If you feel we've got it wrong or left something out, we'd like to know, and if you can remember the address, the price, the phone number, so much the better.

We'll credit all contributions, and send a copy of the next edition (or any other DIRECTIONS guide or Rough Guide if you prefer) for the best letters. Everyone who writes to us and isn't already a subscriber will receive a copy of our full-color thrice-yearly newsletter. Please mark letters: "San Francisco DIRECTIONS Update" and send to: Rough Guides, 80 Strand, London WC2R 0RL, or Rough Guides, 4th Floor, 345 Hudson St, New York, NY 10014. Or send an email to mail@roughguides.com

Have your questions answered and tell others about your trip at www.roughguides.atinfopop.com

Rough Guide credits

Text editor: Shea Dean, April Isaacs
Layout: Ankur Guha
Photography: Maggie Hallahan, Angus Oborn, Nelson Hancock
Cartography: Katie Lloyd Jones

Picture editor: Helen Stallion
Proofreader: Sarah Hull
Production: Aimee Hampson
Design: Henry Iles
Cover design: Chlöe Roberts

SMALL PRINT

The author

Mark Ellwood moved to America from England in 1998 and has lived out of a suitcase ever since, zigzagging from Washington State to Washington DC. On the way, among other things, he's learnt how to make shoo-fly pie and visited an all-psychic town. Mark is co-author of several other Rough Guides, including Miami and California, and also writes regularly on fashion and travel for various magazines. He Lives in New York City.

Acknowledgments

Thanks above all to Tim Zahner at the San Francisco CVB, who's never failed to find an answer to even my most obscure questions and continues to have patience with my endless requests; also to his colleagues Laurie Armstrong and Geraldine O'Brien for their willing input. Thanks also go to Patty Kahn, Paul Frentsos, Patricia Darden, Kelly Chamberlin, Katie Williams, Charles Zukow, Susan Wilson Tom Walton, Paul Frentsos, Patty Kahn, Courtney Vaughn and Pieter Ruig, Jared Rivera and Teresa Piro, without whose help my trip would have been far less fun. Deep thanks to Dawn Shalhoup, Allison Goldstein, Guy Muzio and Lori Puccinelli Stern, each of whom has proved an invaluable source of information on insiders' San Francisco. On a personal note, thanks to Virginia Cartwright and Alison Diboll, adoptive San Franciscans who make my every trip there a joy; and to Rachel Brown, Letizia Treves and Addison Marshall, each of whom have joined me on research trips and helped shape my impressions through a new set of eyes. Back at Rough Guides HQ, thanks to April Isaacs and Shea Dean for their smart, sharp-eyed editing, and to Andrew Rosenberg for asking me to take on San Francisco in the first place. And thanks, as ever, to Maureen, Ben and Jason who kept the home fires burning while I was gallivanting round California.

Photo credits

All images © Rough Guides except the following:

p.8 Grant Avenue © Chuck Pefley/Alamy
p.10 Union Square © DK Images
p.11 Alcatraz, D Block © DK Images
p.12 Japanese Tea Garden © DK Images
p.13 Strybing Arboretum © Bruce Peters/California Horticultural Society
p.14 Washington Square © Morton Beebe/Corbis
p.15 Fort Mason Center © Fort Mason Center/Ronald Tierney
p.15 Yoda Statue © The Presidio Trust
p.15 Mission Dolores Park © Danita Delimont/Alamy
p.17 Archbishop's Mansion © Russell Abrahams
p.17 Hotel Des Arts © Hotel Des Arts
p.17 Hotel Vitale © Hotel Vitale
p.19 The Castro © Catherine Karnow/Corbis
p.19 Stud Bar © Stud SF
p.19 GLBT © GLBT Historical Society
p.21 Amoeba Records © Amoeba Records

p.22 California Palace of the Legion of Honor © Fine Arts Museum of San Francisco
p.23 de Young Museum © Fine Arts Museum of San Francisco
p.24 Tin How Temple © DK Images
p.24 Grace Cathedral © DK Images
p.25 St Mary's Cathedral © DK Images
p.25 Church of St Peter & Paul © Saints Peter and Paul Church
p.28 Halloween on the Castro © Ed Kashi/Corbis
p.28 Chinese New Year © David R. Frazier Photolibrary, Inc./Alamy
p.29 Gay Pride © Justin Sullivan/Getty Images
p.29 Cherry Blossom Festival © Richard Cummins/Corbis
p.29 Cinco de Mayo dancers © Morton Beebe/Corbis
p.31 Dim Sum © David Sanger Photography/Alamy
p.32 The Canvas © The Canvas

Selected images from our guidebooks are available for licensing from:

ROUGHGUIDESPICTURES.COM

SMALL PRINT

p.33 Vino Venue © Vino Venue

p.33 Voda © Voda

p.35 San Francisco Symphony © San Francisco Symphony/Kristen Loken

p.35 Beach Blanket Babylon © SSPI 2006 Photo by David Allen

p.36. Luella © Luella

p.36 Taylor's Automatic Refresher © Douglas Sterling

p.38 Nook © Nook

p.40 Chinatown night market © SanFrancisco Chinatown.com

p.41 The Globe © The Globe

p.42 Reverend Cecil Williams at Glide Memorial Church © Kevin Fleming/Corbis

p.43 Baker Beach © DK Images

p.43 Take a city Guides walking tour © www .sfcityguides.org

p.44 Myth © Myth

p.45 Ferry Building Market Place © Ferry Building

p.45 Greens © Greens Restaurant

p.45 Chez Panisse © Clarissa Horowitz

p.46 Jonathan Sanchez of the San Francisco Giants © MLB Photos/Getty Images

p.51 Mezzanine © Nino-Eduardo C. Palana/ Mezzanine Photos

p.51 Mighty © Mighty

p.52 Topless waitressing © Kim Kullish/Corbis

p.53 Fortune Cookies © RF/Corbis

p.53 Vegetable and Beef Chop Suey © mediacolor's/Alamy

p.55 Defenestration outdoor wall © Brian Goggin

p.56 Good Vibrations © 2004 Good Vibrations, photo by Phyllis Christopher

p.57 Bay to Breakers Race © Cindy Chew

p.58 University of California campus © Mark E. Gibson/Corbis

p.59 View of city from Alcatraz © Golden Gate National Recreation Area/NPS

p.61 Mark Twain © Mary Evans Picture Library/ Alamy

p.64 San Francisco coastline © DY Riess MD/Alamy

p.86 Tai Chi in Washington Square © SFCVB/Mark Downey

p.87 Café Trieste © Café Trieste

p.94 Lombard Street © Ron Watts/Corbis

p.100 The Cannery © Courtesy of The Cannery at Del Monte Square

p.109 The Warming Hut © Maggie Hallahan

p.116 The SFMOMA © San Francisco Museum of Modern Art

p.118 Losts Arts Salon © Lost Arts Salon

p.129 Suite One8One © Suite One8One

p.141 Castro Theatre © Christian Horan

p.152 de Young Museum © San Francisco Museum of Modern Art

p.160 Holocaust Memorial © Danita Delimont/ Alamy

p.161 Cliff House restaurant ruins of Sutro Baths © Stephen Saks Photography/Alamy

p.174 Paramount Theatre © Oakland CVB

p.180 Mt. St. Helena, Napa Valley © Brent Miller/ winecountry.com

Index

Maps are marked in color

INDEX

INDEX

WHEREVER YOU ARE,

WHEREVER YOU'RE GOING,

WE'VE GOT YOU COVERED!

Rough Guides Travel Insurance

Visit our website at www.roughguides.com/insurance or call:

- ☎ UK: 0800 083 9507
- ☎ Spain: 900 997 149
- ☎ Australia: 1300 669 999
- ☎ New Zealand: 0800 55 99 11
- ☎ Worldwide: +44 870 890 2843
- ☎ USA, call toll free on: 1 800 749 4922

Please quote our ref: *Rough Guides books*

Cover for over 46 different nationalities and available in 4 different languages.